Believing Beyond!

A journey from unbelief to great Faith

Written by

Regina Ravenell-Carr

Regina Ravenell-Carr
New York, NY

Disclaimer
Names, characters, places, and incidents either are the product of the author's imagination or are used fictitiously, and any resemblance to actual persons, living or dead, business establishments, events, or locales is entirely coincidental.

Unless otherwise stated, all Scripture has been quoted from the New King James Version of the Bible as cited on www.biblegateway.com

Cover - Editing- Interior Layout: Robin E. Devonish, the Self-Publishing Maven

Formatting: Joy E. Turner, JetSet Communications & Consulting

ISBN 13: 978-0997380903

ISBN 10: 099738090X

Printed in the United States of America

<u>Acknowledgements</u>

To God be the glory, for the great things
that He has done!

To my husband and my children

Thank you for the privilege of being in your
lives, for seeing me through every test and
every trial, and allowing me to become the
Woman of God, I was purposed to be. May
the Christ that lives in me live in you too!

To my Dad and my sister

You are the wind beneath my wings!

To my co-workers and friends

Thank you for listening, sharing, critiquing,
encouraging, supporting and believing in
me.

To the members of my ministry

Christian Uprise Thru Edification Discipleship Ministry, Inc.

You are the best!

My extended church family

Apostle Dr. Patricia Wiley and The Oil of Joy
Ministries II, Inc.

Your prayers, power, and praise kept me
connected to the Vine!

Love you all for all that you've done!

Contents

Introduction

Has God spoken to you in various ways and at different times? If so, that has happened to me as well. I think we can agree that it can be hard to comprehend the vision God has deposited into our spirit. Perhaps, you have been sidetracked from arriving to your purpose and your destiny. And that distraction has resulted in you becoming discouraged and frustrated. In those times, it is difficult to imagine how you will get from where you are to where you "believe," you are supposed to be!

In my years of ministering, I have come to learn that many people search, looking for fulfillment, love and purpose in all the wrong places. What is the wrong place? I say anywhere outside of ourselves and outside of God's way. The work that God does happens on the inside, not on the outside. So, the search should be connected to our spiritual life that God has already ordained for us! I learned this the hard way, and that is the way, most of us learn what we learn.

Drowning in despair, I dug deeper into the things of God, to find my purpose and His plan for my life. I am so excited because this book is an opportunity for me to share the many experiences that brought me to a new place in God, in my marriage, and in my ministry.

During my spiritual journey, I have identified the greater need for believers, and possibly non-believers, to exercise our faith to overcome our issues and leap into our destiny.

This book is not a counseling session because we are not diving into your past. I am here to coach you and to challenge you into recognizing where you are and challenge you to take the next and necessary steps to move forward in life. I believe, dear reader, it is my assignment to encourage you, enlighten you, embrace you and edify you to seek after what God has created you to be.

Many never look up to ask, "God, what am I supposed to be doing? "Who am I?" "What is my purpose?" Too many of us are afraid to challenge ourselves to question our purpose because we're fearful of being disappointed by our inability to accomplish it! The good news is that you were not designed to accomplish your purpose in life on your own! God has a plan for you! He wants you to put your trust in Him and have no doubt, and He will direct your path (Proverbs 3:5-6).

Prepare yourself!

We're about to journey together from here, to where we are spiritually ordained to be!

Everyone has a story! Our stories are connected to our divine purpose (purposely) designed by God, for us! Reader, whatever you have been through hasn't destroyed you and God still has desires to use you. Therefore, the time has come for us all to emerge from a "spirit of unbelief," release the shackles of doubt and fear and robe ourselves with the garments of faith provided by God. "Without faith, it is impossible to please God." (Hebrews 11:6)

Reader, I encourage you to believe that your faith is sufficient enough if you activate it and exercise it, according to God's word. As you read this book, my desire is to build up your faith to be convinced beyond any doubt, that you have the ability to fulfill your purpose. And 'its' in your spirit! It's surpassing your understanding and trusting in the Lord. Begin embracing the impact of the power of God that is operating in your life!

Your faith activates God's virtue, and His virtue will empower you to overcome any issues. Therefore, whatever issues you are facing, He is using them as your refining fire. We will show you that God already has the plan to deliver you, but your faith has to be your substance while you are going through it! We want you to know that the water is only three feet deep, and you are not going to drown. He is using you to show others that His will is good, it is perfect, and it is acceptable. He is using your story to edify (to instruct morally, to teach), others, by your faith! We are building you up so that you will be able to build up others. God promises, that after you have endured for a little while, you will receive a just reward (Hebrews 10:36).

"Believing Beyond," simply wants you to give attention to the "dangers of unbelief, of neglect, and drifting away." There's no reason to turn away from your faith! I am challenging you to "hold on to your confessions," of Jesus Christ; go toward spiritual maturity and not turn back." There are several exhortations that we will address in this book, to hear the voice of God and repent.

After each chapter, you will find a passage called, "My Story, My Voice!" It's a glimpse of my journey from a spirit of unbelief to great faith. I pray that as you journey with me, it will encourage, enlighten, and edify you to move from where you are, to where He has called you to be! I believe my story will connect to your story, and you will find that His truth, His presence, His power and divine will is attainable for you, just like it was attainable for me! We have all been created in His image, to do a greater work than He has done. Your change will bring change to someone else. Yes, someone is waiting for your breakthrough, for their deliverance.

Get ready, get set, and let's go!

A Spirit of Unbelief

"Beware, brethren, lest there be in any of you an evil heart of unbelief in departing from the living God." (Hebrews 3:12 NIV)

How often do we think about doing things beyond our creative abilities? You know what I am talking about, those things that spring up in our spirit? We experience the revelation of ideas and feel the creative juices flowing, but when it's time for the rubber to meet the road, we draw back! How many times have you flushed your visions, your ideas, and your desires down the drain because of your fear of failure? I don't know about you and your experiences with following the revelation of ideas and the flow of creative juices, but I have spent many years being overwhelmed with the anxiety of my fear of failure. Never believing, I was the chosen one! You know, the one who could walk in shoes that fit the person created in my ideas and visions. How could I be the one?

How many times have others told you that you were going to be something, and you completely ignored the thought and the possibility that you could become the some-thing? We accept the negative before we learn to embrace the positive. If you can't see "beyond" what's right in front of you, then you will never reach beyond what is right in front of you.

I could go on and on with questions to get you to see the real point here! But, it's simple! We live in a state of doubt and fear because of our "unbelief!" That's right! You probably don't want to believe that it's unbelief. However, I promise by the end of this book, you will be convinced and even persuaded that your FAITH makes a difference in the quality of your decisions. We will see that as our FAITH grows, so does our ability to see beyond what's in front of us; see beyond what we feel, and beyond what we can imagine in our hearts. "Eye has not seen, nor ear heard, nor have it entered into the heart of man the things that God has prepared for those who love Him." (1 Corinthians 2:9)

You see, what is being deposited into our spirits, by the Power of the Holy Spirit, is strange and peculiar to us. So, we struggle with the new and different because it's something unfamiliar. We look to others to validate the vision because it's beyond our spiritual capacity! But, it's not for them to understand, it's for you, and you only. When you turn to others (your family and friends) for insight on that which is spiritual, you will find they're not equipped or empowered to discern the vision.

We have to learn to search within our soul, be settled in our spirit and embrace it in our mind, what He has in store for us! The plan and purpose that God has for each of us lives on the inside. It may appear to be a mystery that has to be revealed, but it's only a mystery to those that are not seeking to know. The Holy Spirit is here to show it to you, to help you to accept the will of God and to walk by faith and not by sight.

The Holy Spirit helps you to dig deeper and search your heart for the things that God has called you to do! Anyone can attend church (without repentance), give your tithes (out of their disposable cash), and serve on the various auxiliaries (without a personal relationship with Christ). But, everyone is not willing to change their lifestyles or sacrifice their all, to serve the Lord Jesus Christ! Many are called, but few answer the call. Is something stirring on the inside of you? Something that you've been trying to silence and ignore, something that seems to be greater than yourself? God is calling you by your name. "Today, if you will hear His voice, do not harden your hearts as in the rebellion, in the day of trial in the wilderness, as our forefathers did." (Hebrews 4:7)

Prepare yourself!

The spirit of unbelief is subtle. It's not going to stand up and scream to get your attention, but it will cause you to harden your heart against the things of God. When we allow life's struggles, trials and tribulations, disappointments and rejections to consume our thoughts, attitude, and lifestyle, the outcome is that our hearts will harden. We will "assume" the position of caring for one another, however, we won't release our heart to receive and give love! We establish superficial relationships to give the appearance of being connected to others, but our hearts are still cold and disconnected. We make efforts to keep our emotions detached to spare ourselves from disappointment, heartache and pain. We BELIEVE that we are protecting ourselves by being disconnected, and we are safeguarding our possessions. However, I have learned that this false sense of security, also known as a defense mechanism, is only keeping us separated from ourselves and a genuine relationship with Christ and others. My Mother always told me, "If you keep your hand closed too tight, nothing gets in, and nothing gets out." The real consequence is that we are distancing ourselves as opposed to drawing people to us. It hinders us from receiving what God has for us because our hands and hearts are tightly closed! Separation is another trick of the enemy to keep us outside of an intimate and personal relationship with Christ and others. He wants to keep us buried in pain, in grief for the loss of a loved one, in anger and resentment. These characteristics cannot co-exist with the Holy Spirit. You must choose to be set free and not believe the enemy's report, but believe the report of the Lord! Once you find yourself open to Christ, the Holy Spirit will begin to flow like living water. You'll never thirst again. You will recognize and resist the tricks of the enemy and renounce the spirit of unbelief!

The spirit of unbelief will also cause us to drift away from the true and living God! Notice the words "to drift!" That's the subtly of the enemy. He knows that he has to lure you away from God like he lured Adam and Eve! He used his cunningness and trickery to persuade them to turn from and disobey God. Satan builds his case against you by recalling all of your mistakes, disappointments, even the stuff that nobody knows about you. When it looks like all hope has gone, he will zoom in with the voice of unbelief and say, I told you so. Nobody loves you. Nobody cares about you, and no one can help you. He also seduces us with the temptation of the lust of the eyes, the lust of the flesh and the pride of life to draw us away from believing! Lust is an emotion or feeling of intense desire in the body. But, it can take any form; there's more to lusting than just sex. We lust after money, cars, houses, clothes, glamour, success, companionship, and even friendships! The spirit of unbelief opens the door to the three channels of temptation.

I must applaud Dr. Neal T. Anderson, founder of Freedom in Christ Ministries, and president of Discipleship Counseling Ministry. He is also the author of "The Bondage Breaker," and many other books. He introduced me to this understanding and application of the three channels of temptation, found in 1 John 2:15-17. This application gave me such clarity!

The first channel is the "lust of the flesh."

The definition of "lust of the flesh" is having animal appetites, cravings, and passions. Can you identify your animalistic, obsessions, feverish emotions? It could be you are a shopaholic, alcoholic or just infatuated. Whatever is driving you into this frenzy, is driving you away! Yielding to the lust of the flesh will draw us away from God and destroy our dependence upon God. The enemy is looking for your vulnerability in your physical appetites for food, rest, comfort and sex. This temptation is the greatest when hunger, fatigue, and loneliness are present! He's watching you and waiting for you to fall into that weak spot to capture you as prey to a lion. He is waiting to tear you to pieces!

The second channel of temptation is the "lust of the eyes."

The "lust of the eyes" is our selfishness and self-interest. Before we can get to God, our eyes are fixed on ourselves, and the things we desire and expect will meet our needs. We are seduced into the self-gratification of having whatever we want, whenever we want it, at any cost! Spouses have been deserted; children abandoned, homes and cars repossessed, and etc., in the name of selfishness and self-interest. The "lust of the eyes," draw us away from the Word of God, and it destroys our confidence in God. We see what the world has to offer, and we desire it above our relationship with God. We place more credence in out perspective of life than in God's commands and promises! Lust fuels us and then we can't get enough of what we want and what we must have!

The third channel of temptation is, "the pride of life," which is at the heart of temptation.

The "pride of life," is self-promotion and self-exaltation. It is directing our own destiny, ruling our world, and becoming the god of our lives! It's our way or the highway. Only you know what is best, and you dismiss any alternatives to your personal point of view! Unfortunately, the "pride of life," draws us away from the Worship of God and destroys our obedience to God! Whenever you feel you don't need God's help, and you can handle your life without consulting Him, you are in the pride of life! You were created for worship and must beware that you should never stop worshipping and serving God. When you are operating in the pride of life, you are in reality worshipping and serving Satan!

Now, I hope this application is making it clearer, and it helps you to connect with the Holy Spirit on all three levels. I also hope you are convinced and want to break the bondage of the spirit of unbelief. If so, it's time for us to do the work to overcome these three temptations!

It's time to examine yourself!

Pause, breathe and think for just a few moments! Have I allowed the spirit of unbelief to creep its way into my spirit? Have I fallen into the enemy's trap? There's a warning, in the book of Hebrews, which speaks of the danger of neglect (what Christ has already done for you). And the danger of unbelief (to not believe He has saved and delivered you from the hands of the enemy)! The scripture says to beware, which means, to be wary, cautious or careful of; to be on guard. I encourage you to beware of the trick of the enemy. Pay attention, take a good look around, and see who or what is influencing your spirit.

Satan is at his best! What a liar he is! But, the God that I serve says, "He will never leave you nor forsake you." Since Christ is always with you and the Holy Spirit dwells within, there's no way Satan can have his way with you! God already knows what you will go through. He doesn't say that you won't experience hardship, or trials and tribulations, but He does promise to bring you through it all. "For you have a need of endurance so that after you have done the will of God, you may receive the promise." (Hebrews 10:36)

Most of us will believe God for this or for that. But once we get what we want, we revert to being selfish and self-centered. The Bible calls that a temporary faith. If you wish to overcome the spirit of unbelief, your faith has to be greater and deeper, not temporary faith.

Look at the children of Israel who Moses delivered out of Egypt. The Israelites were looking for a redeemer, a deliverer, someone to save them from the hand of Pharaoh. They prayed night and day for God's help. Once Pharaoh obeyed the voice of God and let God's people go, they were still murmuring and complaining, even in the wilderness. While Moses was on the mountain, talking to God, the children of Israel became rebellious. They drifted away! To fall away or drift away from God is to be hardened through the deceitfulness of temptation and sin. We must remember the enemy is always roaming to and fro, seeking who he can devour. He's trying to snatch you from the hand of God. He wants to persuade and convince you to BELIEVE that you are not who God says you are. He wants you to continue to live life wounded, with hurt emotions and pain. Your hurt emotions and pain will keep you in a vulnerable state, unable to see beyond what you think or feel! He wants you to doubt the vision that is in your spirit. He doesn't want you to believe the power that God has already deposited in you. As long as he can keep you outside of the ark of safety, outside of the Will of God, he will have accomplished his mission and aborted your spiritual baby (your purpose). Jesus kept His promise to His Father, and to us; He is still protecting us! He has also promised that He will not allow the enemy to snatch us out of His hand.

The children of Israel wandered away from God, and Satan wants to lure us away from God too! When our needs aren't immediately met, we become discouraged and employ our will to acquire what we desire. We will make graven images out of relationships (the lust of the flesh), tangible possessions (the lust of the eyes), and lustful pleasures (the pride of life). We choose to live according to the things of this world (because we can see it) than to believe what God has in store for us. We become vulnerable to our fears, our anxieties, and our lack of FAITH.

Is there a struggling or wrestling in your spirit because you are attempting to do the "right" thing? Are you always telling yourself no, when God has unequivocally said yes? Are you questioning your ability, your gifts, your vision while looking through (or lusting after) the eyes of others? If you have answered yes to any of these questions, then this book is for you. The time is now for you to take a deeper look at your place in God. Are you living according to your FAITH or according to your fears? Can you see beyond your belief? If so, certainly, God has a way for us to escape the snare of temptation.

It's time to do the work (in my Iyanla Vanzant voice). It's time to come out, come out from wherever you are! Growing up in Brooklyn, NY, I lived in the New York City Housing Authority (NYCHA) Lafayette Gardens development. There was a game we played called "hide-and-seek!" Everyone would run and hide while the person who was "It" would count to 10! When the "It-person," finished counting, they would have to run around to find and catch everybody! While running around, they would shout, "Come out, come out, from wherever you are!" I hear the Holy Spirit calling you out of your hiding place. As in the park where we played, there weren't too many places to hide without being seen. So although we were trying to hide, the "It" person could probably still see us.

God still sees you, and He knows exactly where you are, what you are doing, and He's still calling for you to come out of darkness into His marvelous light. When the "It" person finds you and tags you, you then become part of his team to catch the others! Once you come out of hiding, and the "It" person tags you, you have to change teams. You are now on the other team! Now you have to change your thinking from hiding to being seen!

We would play this game for hours and hours. Everyone probably got a turn to be "It!" It didn't matter how long it took to catch each other, chase each other, and finally tag each other. We enjoyed the time together, developed long-term relationships (that still exist today), and made sure we all had a turn to get to the other side. I hope you can hear me calling you: "Come out; come out from wherever you are." There's new life awaiting you that is beyond a spirit of unbelief, beyond whatever is holding you back from taking this spiritual journey. Jeremiah 29:11, says, "For I know the thoughts that I think toward you, says the Lord, thoughts of peace and not evil, to give you a future and a hope." When you join the other team, the doubts and fears will no longer overtake you. You'll be able to see and believe beyond the dark clouds, beyond the tears, and beyond your past! You'll see your future and hope in Christ Jesus!

As we journey forward, we will further discuss the spirit of unbelief vs. our faith in God. We will see what faith is, how it works in our lives, and how it will bring us to our divine destiny. If you're still stuck here, I want to remind you that Sin will take you further than you want to go. It will also keep you longer than you want to be kept and cost you more than you're willing to pay! So, begin believing that you are more than a conqueror, you are who God says that you are; that what is stirring on the inside of you is real and has a great purpose! You ARE THE ONE, (for such a time as this)! But you have to believe beyond the moment.

My Story...
My voice...

It took a long time to find my voice and to speak in it. I had to journey from a voice of unbelief to a voice of a supernatural faith. I did not believe in myself nor in the voice of the person that others heard. When I began to hear the voice of God, I couldn't imagine that He was calling me! I did not believe I would stand in the gap, where so many others stood. My life was always behind the eight ball; therefore, I was ready to settle for the mediocrity of life. But, I knew I heard Him speaking to me! He seemed to be ushering me out of my comfort zone, into an unfamiliar place of recognition.

I remember sitting in a Sunday service feeling the nudging in my spirit that God wanted me to speak. Immediately, I said to myself, "You have got to be kidding?" I knew I was not "fit" for the Kingdom nor was I smart enough to be an oracle of God, in the fashion I was accustomed. Being chosen by God was out of the question. My spirit of unbelief told me that I could not and would not be, the Woman of God I am today.

Because of my unbelief, I journeyed in a different direction from where God was calling me! I knew He had made a mistake and that there were others that would be better for the job than me. By this time, I am giving birth to my second child, leaving their father, and struggling to find my real identity in this world! I'm sure you can imagine the twist and turns I've had to endure, to try to find ME.

In 1989, a friend gave me the Open Book Bible" as a birthday present. I began to study the Word (according to the Christian's Guide to Christian Living), and I can honestly say that my life started to change. I would spend hours in the word of God, being awakened to the awesomeness of Him and His word. I gained a zeal for God's wisdom and understanding, my faith increased, and I now believed that He had something greater for me to do.

The power of His word was able to shake my spirit of unbelief, and it delivered me to a state of great faith. I believed God that I was not who "I," thought I was; but "greater is He that is within me, than he that is in the world." My new found faith gave me a new love that I never knew before! I was ready to embrace the experience by faith!

<u>Restoring Your Faith</u>

"But without FAITH it is impossible to please Him, for he who comes to God must believe that He is, and He is a rewarder of those who diligently seek Him." (Hebrews 11:6)

FAITH! What is it? And, is my faith good enough?

FAITH is a word that means so many things to so many different people! Faith is freely given to all, but we all fail to receive the gift as it has been freely given. Faith challenges our very being. It causes us to be tested and tempted, sometimes before we have a clear understanding of what or who we believe. We have developed a false sense of faith, without having complete knowledge or understanding of it. The book of James tells us "faith without works, is not faith!" Faith without works is dead, and a dead faith is worse than no faith at all. It says, "Faith must produce; it must be visible. Verbal faith is not enough; mental faith is insufficient. It inspires action!"

In our journey to "believing beyond," we must begin seeing the enemy for whom the word says he truly is! He is the Prince of this world and the Father of lies! Therefore, anything that comes from him is evil and deceitful. Do you recall his role in the Garden of Eden? He tricked Eve and Adam, to eat the forbidden fruit. God gave the command to Adam saying, "Of every tree of the garden you may freely eat, but of the tree of the knowledge of good and evil you shall not eat, for in the day that you eat of it, you shall surely die" (Genesis 2:16). A few verses later, you find the serpent having a conversation with Eve. The serpent says to Eve, "has God indeed said, 'You shall not eat of every tree of the garden?'" And there it is, the trick of the enemy! Eve's curiosity has been peaked and then the serpent goes in for the kill when he says, "Surely you will not die!" So, Eve ate the forbidden fruit and gave it her husband; he ate too! And the consequence was a curse, because of their disobedience and unbelief. They did not believe the word and promises of God! Hence, their sin has become our sin! Their spirit of unbelief has become our spirit of unbelief!

To overcome the spirit of unbelief (that we discussed in chapter one), we have to understand who and what faith is. Why? Because faith is the only action we can take to dispel the spirit of unbelief. Whatever is in your spirit, is what is going to come out. You are what you eat! If you possess a lying spirit, then you will tell lies. A spirit of unbelief comes from Satan (John 8:43-47) and is caused by sin (John 16:9)! Unbelief also manifests when we doubt God, His Word, and His promises to us! So you see, to overcome the spirit of unbelief and fill the void, "Faith" must have a constant refueling in your life.

You have to put your faith to work to fight the demonic spirit that comes to steal, to kill and to destroy! Adam and Eve lived in a garden where everything was good and pleasant. They allowed the serpent to deceive them and lost all rights and privileges afforded to them. They were cursed and driven out of the garden to till the ground!

The serpent is still at work today! His desire is to take you out; to cancel your assignment, to dismiss your purpose and to black out your vision. Are you willing to be defeated by that old, ugly, adversary? Are you willing to let him take you down and get you thrown out? I hope not! He has no power and can only tempt you with temptation. Choose you this day whom you will serve!

By faith, I believe right now, you have chosen to renounce the spirit of unbelief and pursue a spirit of FAITH!

The Merriam-Webster dictionary defines faith as strong belief or trust in someone or something; belief in the existence of God: strong religious feelings or beliefs. If this book was for the carnally-minded, this definition might suffice. But, as believers, we have to identify who and in what we believe. First, we must confess our faith, firmly believe in Jesus Christ, and that He is the living

Son of God. Then, we would have to declare that we believe the Word of God, as the foundation of our faith.

This definition might seem elementary to some, but I want to be as simple and transparent as possible for the believer who has just accepted Christ and is looking for inspiration, encouragement, instruction, and direction. Because you have just begun this journey, you need to be encouraged that your life is changed because you have received the Lord by faith. Faith is a new road that you will travel, and some of the seeds that God has for you may take longer to spring forth than others, but don't give up! Be patient in the seedling time. They're the seeds the Holy Spirit is pouring into you. You must be prepared for the pruning and growth process. The pruning is the tearing off of the unnecessary (carnal) things, and the growing will be the presence of the Holy Spirit birthing some (spiritual) things into you. You are being transformed!

There's also a population of believers I am seeking after that I will refer to as the "middle of the road society." Jesus describes them in the parable of the soils:

In Mark 4:3-7, we find "the farmer went out to sow his seed, and some fell on rocky places, where it didn't have much soil." It, the seed (we will refer to the seed as your faith), sprang up quickly because the soil was shallow. But when the sun came up, the plants were scorched, and they withered because they had no root. Your faith was scorched because it was not rooted and grounded in the word of God. Because you sprang up so quickly, there was not enough of God's word coupled with your faith to sustain you and allow you to be rooted (connected) to the vine of Jesus Christ. You are still important to God, and your faith can be restored. You can get back in line. It's not too late for you to grow and flourish! Receive the love of God, allow Him into your heart to refresh and restore you back to the place He has for you!

There is another group that is being summoned that I would like to call the "throne-bearing people." In this group are those "whose seed fell among the thorns, which grew up and choked the plants, so that they did not bear grain." In this case, the believer has taken their eyes off the mark and failed to tend to the ground where the thorns were growing. They allowed the thorns (the things of this world), to overtake the spiritual seeds planted!

In the beginning, did you have a passion and zeal to serve the Lord? Something has happened to you, and you have become sedated by life! Is it by disappointment, by heartache, by the loss of loved ones, by financial difficulties and so on? Has your faith been choked, or your joy stolen? Does it feel like the enemy is killing you softly, and your spirit is being destroyed? If so, it's time for you to fight back by faith. It's time to "resist the enemy, and he will flee from you. Draw near to God, and He will draw near to you (James 4:7)."

Come on, let's go up!

Faith is not only a profession about Christ, but it also requires action that comes from the heart of the believer who seeks to follow Him! The action required, is found in Romans 10:9-10. "That if you confess with your mouth the Lord Jesus and believe in your heart that God has raised Him from the dead, you will be saved. For with the heart, one believes to righteousness, and with the mouth confession is made to salvation." The two actions required to activate your faith is to confess and believe.

To confess means to admit that you've done something wrong against God. Also, to be honest enough to tell God that you have done wrong. The Bible also uses the word confession to describe an open, bold, and courageous proclamation of one's faith. In Matthew 16, Jesus asks the disciples, "Who do you say that I am?" The disciple's confession of faith is the foundation Christ built His church. Not on sand, clay, or stone, but upon our belief in Him.

When we confess our sins, we public-
ly declare our belief in Christ. Our faith in
Christ will bring us to a place of repentance,
and we will ask for forgiveness. The result is
a sweet release and a welcoming healing to
our souls. Once we confess, it restores our relationships and often brings blessings. Confession is good for the soul, but sometimes it
is difficult! However, it will always work out
for our good. Have you ever committed a sin
that you have tried to hide? Have you ever
sinned against someone and not asked forgiveness? Christ offers us the opportunity to
confess our sins and our faith in the power
of His Holy Spirit. If you have picked up this
book called, "Believing Beyond," you must be
ready and willing to take this journey to a
Christ-centered, abundant and exalted life.
When we confess with our mouth, we will
reap the blessing of having fellowship with
Him and our heart will be purged from all
unrighteousness!

I want to encourage you to begin confessing your sins and your faith to God. The
enemy tricks us into thinking we can hide
from God when that is impossible. His presence is everywhere; He knows everything'
and He has all power in His hand! You don't
have to start from scratch with your story
because He already knows you. He has allowed your life experiences and emotions to
shape you and build your character. Confessing unto the Lord sets us free from the spirit

of heaviness. Talking to God helps us to see ourselves, helps us to confess our sins and helps us to accept what He has for us. "If we confess our sins, He is faithful and just to forgive us our sins and to cleanse us from all unrighteousness!" (1 John 1:9) He continues to sit on the throne of mercy, at the right hand of God, interceding on our behalf! Jesus desires to have fellowship with us, and has made a way for us to escape to the tricks of the enemy. However, we must confess with our mouth and believe in our heart!

The second part of the required action is to believe with your heart! This act must be rooted deeply and firmly in the heart of man and it cannot be a superficial. In the Bible, all emotions are experienced by the heart.

Love	1 Peter 4:8
Hate	Leviticus 19:17
Joy	Psalm 19:8
Sorrow	Psalm 13:2
Peace	Numbers 6:26
Bitterness	Proverbs 14:10
Courage	Joshua 1:9
Fear	Exodus 20:20

The thinking processes of man are said to be carried out by the heart. Proverbs 23:7 says, "For as a man thinks in his heart, so is he." Faith is a matter of the heart. We must open our hearts to receive the gospel of Jesus Christ and to believe that He is Lord! The heart is the center of the believer. When the Lord sent Samuel to Jesse's house to anoint the next king, He said to Samuel, "Do not look at his appearance or the height of his stature, because I have refused him. For the Lord does not see as man sees; for man looks at the outward appearance, but the Lord looks at the heart." (1 Samuel 16:7) Jesus says, "He who believes in Me, as the Scripture has said, out of his heart will flow rivers of living water (John 7:38)." The heart is the wellspring of life. Our faith has to be heart-centered for it to change our mind and our thinking. When we open our heart to the Son of God, He will draw nigh to us. Ezekiel 36:26 says, "I will give you a new heart and put a new spirit within you; I will take the heart of stone out of your flesh and give you a new heart of flesh!"

God has promised to restore Israel, you, and the living church! He promises to change our heart from a heart of stone (evil, angry, troubled and hard) to a heart of flesh (loving, courageous, repentant, delighted and humbled).

Jesus still loves you! Like he loved the adulterous woman who was exposed to "Him," for embarrassment and stoning. Jesus said, "Let he who is without sin cast the first stone." We don't have to hide our sins if we allow the Holy Spirit to overtake us and cleanse us from all unrighteousness. You still have a purpose and God still has a use for you. David had to realize that he had sinned against God and had to cry out to the Lord for forgiveness. He cried, "Purge me with hyssop, and I shall be clean; wash me, and I shall be whiter than snow. Create in me a clean heart and renew the right spirit within me. Break my bones and make them anew; Restore unto me, the joy of my salvation." (Psalms 51) You may have fallen, but you can get back up!

"Today, if you hear his voice, do not harden your hearts as they did in the rebellion, during the time of testing in the wilderness!"

Christ came for us to have life and to have it more abundantly! The Old Testament children missed their opportunity for their abundant life because they did not obey God. They failed to add their faith to the promises of God. They had a temporary faith. They believed God for their exodus out of Egypt, but became disobedient in the desert. If you want to get beyond your desert place and arrive at the state of an abundant and exalted life, your heart has to be right. Faith must have an anchor in your heart. If you allow your heart to become hardened with bitterness, resentment, anger, envy and strife, your journey will be unsuccessful. Proverbs 4:23, "above all else, guard your heart, for it is the wellspring of life." Whatever is in you, is what is going to come out. Your life is at stake! Your spiritual life is at stake! Are you in need of a pacemaker or a heart transplant? The Holy Spirit is available to change your heart right now! If you confess with your mouth and believe with your heart!

Once you confess with your mouth and believe with your heart, you will reap the benefit of being in Christ. Your faith will open the heart of God! "Without faith, it is impossible to please God." (Hebrews 11:6)   Pleasing God should be the desired posture of every believer, as well as, touching the heart of God. To please God is to be thoroughly satisfying and diligent toward Him. Being fully satisfying is the greatest degree or extent of meeting a need, or fulfill the need. Our relationship with Christ should be complete with our presence, prayers, obedience, and commitment. He desires us to be faithful to Him, in all things. We can only please Him with a sincere heart. God has promised to pour His Spirit upon us, to equip and empower us to complete the task. Nothing should separate us from what He has given us to do, in His name. We can only please Him with a sincere heart.

One of my favorite restaurants is "The Cheesecake Factory." One Saturday afternoon, a   friend and I, were on our way home from a church service and decided to go out for dessert at "The Cheesecake Factory." I had the warm apple crisp! Can I just tell you that I thought it was the best warm apple crisp I ever had! It was served on a large platter, with the right amount of apple crisp warmed to the right temperature, with caramel drippings, and vanilla ice cream, I ate every drop! It was fully satisfying! It hit the spot and fulfilled every one of my expectations. Eating this dish, was a delightful experience. I highly recommended this dessert to others and suggested that they try it the next time they visited "The Cheesecake Factory!" On another trip, this same friend and I went to see the Broadway musical, "After Midnight!" The music and the performances were excellent! I found the singers to be outstanding, and the dancing was phenomenal. We sang along, tapped our feet, and were mesmerized by the glamor of the show. It thoroughly entertained us. The same way that we have great expectations in the natural to be fully pleased, God has an expectation for us to be fully pleasing to Him. If our desire is to please God with our faith, then we must put our best foot forward with our actions! Our ministry's motto is: "Life without a deep relationship is empty; life without deep spiritual relationship is stagnant!" You can no longer afford to be stagnant; it's time to be diligent (attentive and persistent), in your relationship with God and believe by exercising your faith. You must be pleasing unto Him. You must seek that which He desires like I desired the warm apple crisp!

Psalms 46:1, tells us "God is a very present help in the time of trouble." If we can believe that He is always present when we need Him, then we should be more conscious of His presence in our lives at all times. He is the author and the finisher of our faith. He created us in His image. Therefore, our character should be a constant reminder of who God is in us. We should be distinguishable from the unbeliever because we are of Christ, the true and living Son of God! He does not want us to fade into the background; He wants our light to shine before men.

God is a rewarder! But we must diligently seek Him. We have to put one foot in front of the other and begin to seek after the things of God. To seek after is to be actively engaged in prayer and studying the Word of God. Everyone likes being rewarded for doing well! Don't you want to hear Him say, "You are a good and faithful servant?" Be diligent in your faith! Believing that, HE is! That He does exist and is present in your life. What is your reward? His joy and presence in your life. His shield of protection from the enemy! The enemy can't snatch you out of His hand!

Your faith is necessary! Your faith is good enough! Here's what I want to pour into your spirit right now! By faith, you are saved! Your faith in the Lord Jesus has set you free from the bondage of sin! Your faith has brought you to this place. The Holy Spirit is at work on the inside of you, and your heart is being changed from a heart of stone into a heart of flesh. Believe that your life is being changed! No matter what the enemy wants to convince you of, your life has been changed! Your faith is good enough! Moreover, you are more than a conqueror, and you are already victorious! There's no need to battle with the spirit of unbelief. "You, dear friend, must build yourselves up in your most holy faith, in the Holy Spirit. Keep yourselves in God's love as you wait for the mercy of our Lord to bring you to eternal life." (Jude 20-21NIV)

Faith works! It just requires our actions! I just had a vision of you opening your heart and your spiritual mind to receiving the gift of faith in God. Don't be afraid to unwrap and release your faith! It is a new season and a new day! A dead faith will profit you nothing, but your active faith will please God and He will reward you!

"Believing beyond" your circumstances, disappointments, fears and loss can only be accomplished by faith! When God sees your faith, He responds with His love, His peace, His joy, and His compassion. That's when you will feel a greater sense of His presence in your life. He will light up your life; He will quench your thirst; He'll feed you until you want no more. He will perform miracles, signs and wonders in your life because of your faith. He will equip and empower you to carry out the assignment that He has for your life. You will be rooted, grounded and not be scorched when the sun comes up. The thorns will not choke you because you're established in the kingdom, and you will be able to overcome the attack of the enemy! Christ promises that He won't allow the enemy to snatch you out of His hand! Everything that you have been through has been your refining fire for your divine purpose. The shoestrings of your thoughts will be tied together, and you will have clarity of your purpose. The vision will be crystal clear!

It's time for your exodus! As we walk out of this chapter, I would like to encourage you to confess that you are walking out of the spirit of unbelief and walking in faith. Confessing with your mouth that Jesus is Lord, and believing with your heart that God has raised Him (and you), from the dead! Leave the dead stuff behind you! Don't look back because your greater is coming!

My Story...

My Voice...

I'm awake now, and I have a voice. The more I read God's word, the more I shared it; the more I shared it, the more I could hear Him speaking to me and through me. My confidence in His word was growing and arousing me to rise out of my insecurities, my brokenness, and emptiness. The mediocrity I accepted was no longer acceptable, and change was inevitable.

The change was, I no longer doubted myself; I was putting my trust in God. I began taking giant steps forward by exercising my 'Faith'. Exercising my faith, gave me the ear to hear the voice that the Lord had given to me. It was a new voice that wasn't afraid and was compassionate to the needs others. It also became a voice of reason and a voice of truth. My new voice worshiped the Lord at all times, and His praise is continually in my mouth.

I used this new voice to confess my sins and to declare my faith in God! I could speak life in the midst of my storms, call things that were not as though they were, and learned to hold my peace (my tongue), to let the Lord fight my battles. "Even when my enemies came to eat up my flesh, they stumbled and fell. Though an army should encamp against me, my heart shall not fear. Though war should rise against me, in this will I be confident." (Psalms 27:2-3)

The new voice was a gift from God! It called me out of my darkness into His marvelous light. My head was lifted up, and I was ready to go wherever He led me. A family member once told me that she could hear the sound of my trumpet. I was impressed because I wasn't speaking, but she discerned my spirit. That's a word of encouragement I believe I'll never forget because I am still sounding the trumpet. The road is rough; the going gets tough, and the hills are hard to climb. But, I decided to make Jesus, my choice. I am using my voice to shout from the mountaintop, "that the Lord of love has come to me, and I want to pass it on."

I just couldn't keep it to myself. I was ready to go wherever He sent me! There was a message resonating within that I knew the world needed to hear. I'm grateful to the Joyce Meyers' and the Bishop T.D. Jakes' in the world because it was the sound of their teaching and preaching that made my clarion call to speak His name reign! I got a glimpse of the doors that would be opening, the platforms I would stand on, and the lives I would touch.

<u>My Faith is My Substance</u>

"Now, faith is the substance of things hoped for and the evidence of things not seen." (Hebrews 11:1)

Let's take a deep breath before we press on! Now, exhale! There is a great exhilaration that comes with having your faith activated! By faith, we are walking· into a new dimension, and it is an uphill journey. Paul said, "When I was a child, I spoke as a child, I understood as a child, I thought as a child; but when I became a man, I put away childish things." (1 Corinthians 13:11) What he was saying is, it's time to let go of childish ways and grow in the things of God. Now we understand and are no longer blinded by wrath, anger, bitterness, evil speaking, and malice. And, since our faith has been awakened, we can no longer be children being tossed to and fro (Ephesians 4:14). Paul acknowledges that his speech, understanding, and thoughts, were immature until he came to a full knowledge of Christ. He is encouraging us, as believers, to grow in our faith, to serve Christ and build up the kingdom.

Paul enlightens the church with the understanding that the Lord gave gifts. God gave, "Apostles, Prophets, Evangelists, Pastors, and Teachers, for the equipping of the saints, the work of the ministry, and the edifying of the body of Christ." (Ephesians 4:11-

12). The gifts are for us, to help us build up our faith. Christ also wants us to grow others, according to the gift that He has given. Therefore, the vision inside you is connected to the ministry and purpose that God has ordained for you. However, you won't accomplish your vision without your faith! Right now, there should be no hesitation! We've already dispelled the spirit of unbelief and declared that "your" faith has been restored, and it is sufficient for your journey! So let's, buckle up our shoes, fasten our seat belt and prepare our hearts for this supernatural move!

First, to the "middle of the road" society. You know who you are! The believer whose seed fell on stony ground and sprung up with no root. When the sun came, it scorched you, and you have dried up! I had some plants in my home that have endured some similar conditions. I found that I was treating my plants the way that my life was treating me. Whenever I was "happy," and things seemed to be going well, I would regularly water my plants, and make sure they were exposed to the sun as needed. However, when things weren't good, I would forget about the plants and they would not be watered nor exposed to the sun properly. While wrestling with the spirit, the Holy Spirit dealt with me regarding my spiritual state. He told me that I had to get it together before I lost everything. "I had to strengthen that which remain because it was about to die."(Revelations 3:2). I felt I had already lost the battle, but my spirit was awakened! I began pulling myself together; took a good look around and started strengthening whatever I could in my house. My plants were wilting, scorched, and some were all dried up. I started attending to the plants, with the motivation to restore them. Before I knew it, the plants were coming back to a healthy life! As the plants were being restored, so was I! And, God wants to restore you to a healthy spiritual life too. You are being revitalized with a spiritual relationship with the Lord. Lying dormant, in a sun-dried state is no longer an option. You have to strengthen that which remains in you! Being strengthened means you are given added strength or greater power! Paul prays that we would be "strengthened with might; that we would be rooted and grounded in love" (Ephesians 3:16-17) Prophet Isaiah declares to us the Word of the Lord, "Fear not, for I am with you; be not dismayed, for I am, your God. I will strengthen, yes; I will help you. I will uphold you with My righteous right hand." (Isaiah 41:10) To receive this deposit, you must open your heart and your hand to the Spirit of the Lord! I heard a long time ago, "anything that is dead needs to be resurrected!" I'm encouraging you to believe, you must live and not die.

I'm also reaching out to the "thorn-bearing people." Your life journey has caused you to endure some thorny patches. Your spirit has been scratched and wounded by the thorns of life. You may be feeling choked up from your labor in the vineyard. Is it possible that you've been busy achieving and not busy believing? You may have allowed your "busyness" to occupy you and influence you! The prickles have choked the growth of your spiritual life, and there are no crops. Well, I think I need to introduce you to Sister Martha, the sister of Lazarus and Mary. Jesus is visiting Martha and Mary, at their home. Martha is busy preparing food, setting the table, and the list of her duties goes on! She *commands* Jesus, to reprimand Mary for just sitting at His feet and not helping her with her busy work. Martha determined what was important at that time. Martha is just busy doing what she thinks is right! However, Jesus rebukes Martha for not being like Mary and for allowing the busy work to distract her from the real work. You need to know that your gift is not greater than the Gift! Mary was sitting at the feet of Jesus, hearing the words of Him; that was being deposited into her spirit. Mary knew what she needed in her life and knew that He was her Messiah! Can you put down your "busy" and sit at the feet of Jesus? Are you in tune with His words, His message, His love, wisdom, and understanding? It's time for you to decide, what is your substance? What is preoccupying your spirit? Will you continue to live being busy and not believe beyond your busy-ness? Or, are you willing to, "be not conformed to this world, but be ye transformed by the renewing of your mind (Romans 12:2)? You see, it's by your faith that you will prove that His will is good, it's perfect, and it's acceptable (Romans 12:2b).

Your faith has to be your substance. Your substance, is what sustains you and will keep you through the storm and the rain. It is what you will hold onto in your darkest hour. It will prevent you from being dried up by the sun and from being choked by the tares of life. Whether you are in the middle of the road or being choked by the thorns, this is the hour of release by the power of the Holy Spirit! Your release is according to your faith. It's time to snatch your loin cloth back from the enemy and no longer be exposed to the elements of the sun or the thorns. If you keep your faith in God, you will live and not die! Notice I did not say survive! Faith is not for those who just want to survive; it is for those who want to walk into the promises of God. He has already promised life, more abundantly. You did not die because there remains a mustard seed of faith in you. So come on, you can do this! Get out of your sun-dried or choked up situations and speak faith. Speak to the mountains, "My faith is my substance!"

You need to be assured and convinced that your faith is your substance. Your substance is your confidence. Your confidence is in Christ Jesus, who is the true author and finisher of your faith. Your faith is present, and it is operating NOW! In spite of what you have gone through to get here, your faith has brought you this far, and it will take you beyond what is right in front of you. Paul prays in Ephesians that you would "be able to comprehend with all the saints, what the width and length and the depth and height of the love of God." (Ephesians 3:18)

I can recall when my substance was not always rooted and grounded in Christ, but rather, in the pleasures of this world. I was lead into the trap of getting high (smoking Marijuana (Mary Jane) aka pot or weed)! I'm calling it a trap because my life became blurred by the deception and the illusions of being high! Looking back, now I can see the impact it had and the consequences of the choices I made! One of my childhood friends, Diane and I, laughed at what we thought gave us substance, but it had no real substance! It did not build our character, it did not give us spiritual enlightenment, and it did not make us any promises for our future! The "high," only lasted for a moment, and we would have to continue getting high to maintain the sensation! So, what did it truly do for us besides distract us from our God-ordained place in the kingdom? You can't serve two gods! Since the effects of this substance are deception and delusion, we can agree that it comes from the trick of the enemy! It was a drug that kept me withdrawn from myself, my family and my purpose! Someone is resisting this thought; however, when caught in a trap, you are bound by the limitations of the trap! You only want to mingle with trap people. You don't want to hear the noise of those that are not in the trap, and you become dull of hearing the truth, in Christ Jesus!

Diane and I have been friends since the first grade. She affectionately calls us, friends from crayons to perfume! Once we turned 50, a few years ago, we became friends from crayons to perfume and beyond! She added the beyond for of all the things that we have endured and overcome. In a recent conversation, I shared the concept of this book and the thought of being preoccupied with the wrong substance.

Here's the revelation that I received from that conversation! My door was open to the trap of the enemy because of the attack on my family. My brother, the youngest of three, had been diagnosed with a brain tumor. My parents spent three years, around the clock at the hospital, praying their son would get well! As the middle child, I probably felt neglected by their absence. In the 70s, health care was not as advanced as it is today; therefore, my brother endured great hardships and pain! I remember my Dad telling me stories about how he had to hold Lester's hand while he would be wide-awake, having a spinal tap done. There were many surgeries and periods of rehabilitations he had to go through! Needless to say, Lester died when he was 12 years old, I was 14, and my sister was 18! His death threw our family into despair.

What could restore us! Nothing but the blood of Jesus! My mother began to regain her strength and her faith in God. She began to look up, instead of looking down. She found herself on a spiritual journey, seeking a deeper relationship with her God! It was her spiritual awakening that stirred the rest of us in finding our way back to God. Before Lester passed, he had become a beacon of light. He would testify of being in Christ and letting all of us know that Christ loved each of us too. He was at peace with God! There were times that we would go into his room and know that he had spent time with the Lord! He was my first encounter with the Holy Spirit living on the inside of a person. I believed that Lester had experienced the Christ! I'm speaking this now because when it was time for my life to change, it was Lester's testimony and witnessing my mother's new life that called me out of darkness into His marvelous light! Having a substance of faith, is so great that Satan continues to seek to distract us! Satan knows God has a plan for each of His children. He knows that God has a hedge of protection to sustain us. Faith keeps us on track and in tune with the Word of God and His Holy Spirit! It keeps us connected to the vine!

The vine gives us the spiritual virtue to grow, which is, necessary to increase your faith and receive what God has in store for you! Growing is necessary for you to overcome every obstacle! Growing is necessary for you to bear the fruit of the Spirit and bear witness to the goodness of Jesus and all that He has done! Growing is essential!

My Story...
My Voice...

It's by faith that I made it! Through the storm and the rain, heartache and pain, I never would have made it without Him.

__The Storm__ – it is my faith in God that brings me through every storm I've had to face. Some storms came and went quickly, and others lasted for a while. During the storms is when I find the greatest peace in God. When I think of the years of facing my mother's illness and having to be an encouragement to her, I knew that God was with me! Her illness was a winter season for us. Watching our matriarch transition from being lively, self-sufficient and resourceful, to becoming lethargic, dependent and uninspired was very challenging. In her passing, I remember sharing at her home-going service that she and God had come to an agreement and that I had to accept their decision. My resolve came from the revelation of the Holy Spirit. I heard the Spirit of the Lord say, "Let nothing separate you from the love of God!" Paul says, "For I am persuaded that neither death nor life shall separate us from the love of God which is in Christ Jesus our Lord." (Romans 8:37-39, paraphrased) Because I loved my mother and God, I rested from the labor of her sickness and accepted the will of God.

The Rain – *The Rain came to soften my heart to the things of God. He had to give me a spirit of compassion, forgiveness, joy and peace. It was through my post-honeymoon season that I recognized that I wasn't as forgiving or compassionate as the Holy Spirit was nudging me to be. If I truly wanted to be pleasing unto the Lord and my husband, I had to put my faith in God and allow Him to do the work inside me. In the midst of our most difficult times, I heard the Lord saying, "Peace be still!" I also had to believe the word that says, "Forgive and you will be forgiven!" But what truly blessed and freed me was Jesus told His disciples. "These things I have spoken to you, that my joy may remain in you and that your joy might be full." (John 15:11) He also lets me know, "Peace I leave with you; my peace I give to you. Let not your heart be troubled, neither be afraid." (John 14:27 paraphrased) The early rain allowed God to penetrate my heart with the right kind of spirit to be more obedient to His will and not mine. The latter rain came to grow me and to allow the love of God to establish and perfect me! I received His peace that surpasses all understanding; His wisdom that governs me; and His joy that is my strength!*

The Despair – *I can recall the days of not having hope and overcome by the spirit of fear and doubt. Fear crippled me and doubt had me handcuffed. There were layers of despair that I had to peel off, to find the dia-*

mond that I was created to be. When you are facing the challenges that life brings, the uncertainty of making it through can overwhelm you. When there's no one in your corner, encouraging you to fight on, it can seem impossible that you'll survive to the end! However, I heard the word of the Lord saying, "We are troubled on every side, but not crushed; we are perplexed, but not in despair." (2 Corinthians 4:8) That's when my spirit was relieved! I was no longer puzzled about my brokenness, my weaknesses, or my lowliness. I received light in the midst of my darkness. Many thought I wasn't going to succeed, but God's plan for me was different. I was encouraged during my struggles to believe beyond what I felt and what I saw. I knew this hardship would not last. I had to learn to maneuver strategically around the enemy's attacks against me, my marriage, my children, and my future! The spirit of despair became my fuel for fighting my way out of darkness into His marvelous light. One of the greatest lessons that I learned is, "hurting people hurt people!"

Embracing God's love for me helped me to recognize other's inability to love. So I grew not to allow "their inability to love, to negate my ability to love." The agonies of despair were dispelled and the love that covers a multitude of sin prevailed! That is the love that I have.

It's in the Suffering!

The greatest avenue of attack on the believer is to catch us when we are feeling vulnerable! There are demonic spirits that try to seduce us when we are weak, depressed, and alienated! Does the enemy believe that God is not watching over every one of His children? Satan wants you to think that whatever suffering you are going through or have been through is confirmation that our sovereign God has forsaken us! Once again, he is a liar from the pit of hell! God has not left you! He is a very present help in the time of trouble and a shelter in the time of a storm. Too often, we allow the enemy, and the thinking of this world, to cause us to forsake the promises of God. With our renewed faith, we must know that God is with us in our suffering and that our suffering has a purpose, power, and perfecting! Facing and conquering our difficulties causes us to grow and become strengthened. As we grow, we bring glory to God!

Many are under a grave misconception about the life of the believer! We seem to think or believe that if we confess Christ, we will no longer have to experience hardships, trials and tribulations, loss, heartache, and pain! This kind of thinking opens the door to the enemy's deception. When we can't see God in our suffering, it's not that He is not with us, but that we have taken our eyes off of Him. Sometimes, we are like children who can't see how parents or other guardians protect, provide, and prepare them for life! As a result, they make unwise decisions that often come with great consequences. Once the child experiences the consequence of their bad decision, they begin to see the error of their way. God is present in our suffering, and He has promised to bring us through. As He brings us through, He strengthens us, disciplines us, transforms us, restores us, empowers us and equips us! So, even though Satan is the god of this world, God is still present. God has promised in His Word that "He will not allow us to be tempted beyond what we can bear." (1 Corinthians 10:13)

Everyone knows how precious diamonds are! They are said to be a "girls' best friend!" Moreover, diamonds appeal to men and women because they represent wealth! They come in all shapes, sizes, and colors. Diamonds are very expensive. A tremendous amount of money is spent buying these precious jewels. Well, just as precious as diamonds are to us, we are as precious to Him. Diamonds are formed deep within the Earth, below the surface. A lot of pressure, combined with high temperatures, are necessary to grow diamond crystals. The crystals surface from a very deep-seated, violent volcanic eruption. Our suffering can be seen as the weight of the pressure applied to the earth mixed with the high temperatures required to produce the diamond crystals. When our suffering gets to be overwhelming, that's the violent, volcanic eruption. Without the volcanic eruption, we would not have the diamonds that we've come to value and celebrate. After the diamond has been through its rigorous process, it takes on a life of its own. Although diamonds sparkle and have great sex appeal, they are also strong and enduring. Diamonds appreciate, and they hold their value over time. They are durable, and so are you!

What does all of this mean? You are a diamond!

God sees you in your refined state and knows exactly how much pressure combined with a high temperature you need in your life to produce the quality diamond He has ordained you to be. But, if we don't allow Him to take us through the diamond process, we will never reach the full potential of being a diamond. You will go through life as a knock-off, like a cubic zirconia which is a synthetic gemstone! That means it was artificially produced. The genuine diamond is the strongest stone and is used to sharpen other stones. The diamond can withstand the sharpening without being damaged! It is scratch-proof! The suffering that God allows in your life will not overtake you, but it will cause you to shine by your testimony.

Examples of Suffering

Job, in the Bible, is the perfect example of endurance in adversity. Satan challenged God, to allow him to afflict Job because he thought Job would not be faithful! However, what Satan missed was that God knows the heart of His children, and He already knows who will remain faithful and who will deny Him! So, He allowed Satan to afflict Job. He knew Job would remain faithful, even when he lost everything. Job stayed connected to the God of Abraham, Isaac and Jacob. Job's faith produced God's favor and gave him spiritual authority. For this, he received blessings beyond anything he could ask. You must know and be firmly convinced that God will bless you exceedingly and abundantly above all you can think or even ask when you put your trust in Him! It's in the suffering that we see the authenticity of God!

Suffering by way of Satan

Believers suffer at the hand of the enemy! Satan comes with a host of evil spirits who energize the ungodly, oppose God's will, and frequently attack believers. Are you ready for his attack? Are you equipped to fight this battle of opposition, or, are you prepared for this spiritual warfare? By definition, a spiritual warfare is a battle waged by the power of the Holy Spirit in us. We are at war to resist, overcome and defeat the enemy's lies, deception, temptations and accusations that he sends our way. His attack of temptation follows his lie; then it appeals to our eyes. Deception comes when we believe what's not true. The accusations come to taunt us with our past by rubbing it in our face. Apostle Paul is instructing us, "to be strong in the Lord and the power of His might." To be prepared for this spiritual warfare, you must put on the "whole armor of God." (Ephesians 6:10-18) You can't fight this fight in the natural; you must put on the spiritual armor, use the God-given weapons and pray to persevere and get the victory! It's in the suffering that we overcome the trick of the enemy!

Suffering by way of family

Joseph suffered at the hands of his brothers because of their jealousy (Genensis 37:3-4). They plotted to kill him. But the Lord was with Joseph and Joseph found favor. Despite what Joseph went through, it was part of the divine plan of God. He was preserving Joseph to carry out His purpose to preserve the people of Israel and to unite them together again. We cannot be discouraged when people wage their war against us. Joseph faced rejection, separation, and isolation because of his brothers! However, God had a plan and a purpose for his suffering. He wants to bring you out just like He brought Joseph out! Joseph went from being the victim to the Victor! It's in the suffering that we become victorious!

Do you trust God in the midst of your testing? Newsflash! God can and does use the suffering of the righteous, to further the cause of His Kingdom and His plan for salvation and redemption. Everything Job and Joseph experienced was part of God's plan.

Suffering by way of righteousness

When we suffer for righteousness sake, we build our spiritual character, strengthen our faith in God, and sustain the power of God in the earth. When we trust God in the midst of our storms, he equips and empowers us with the ability to overcome the adversity. Isaiah 54:17 says, "No weapon formed against you shall prosper and every tongue that rises against you in judgment, you will condemn. This is the heritage of the servants of the Lord, and their righteousness is from Me, Says the Lord."

Look up and see God. He is your Deliverer, your Repairer, and Restorer! He will bring forth a great deliverance in your life too. Remember, God has a divine plan for each and every one of us while we are going through our storms. Say it with me, my suffering is not in vain. My suffering has a divine purpose. My suffering is perfecting me. My suffering is preserving a remnant in the earth and because of my suffering, my great deliverance is coming!

Suffering by way of Sin

We also suffer because we live in a sinful and corrupt world of immorality. We are still challenged with the responsibility of being steadfast in God. We all fall short, make wrong turns, and land in a mess. The consequences of our shortcomings bring suffering. Without Christ, our comeback would be endless! David says, "Many are the afflictions of the righteous, but the Lord will deliver them out of them all!" (Psalms 34:19) When I examined this type of suffering, I thought of the woman with an alabaster flask of fragrant oil. (Matthew 26:6-13). Although she is said to be a sinner, wasting extravagant oil, Jesus applauds her for being in the right place, at the right time, doing the right thing. She is a woman of action, in spite of her tears. I believe she needed to reach Jesus, and her need was greater than the possible ridicule of the Pharisees and others. She came prepared to make an ultimate sacrifice of breaking the seal of her alabaster flask and pouring out her expensive oil. Her love for Jesus and His message of salvation brought her to a deep expression of sorrow, grief and a grateful love for Him. The expensive oil she poured out was worth a year of wages. Her act of great sacrifice and loving devotion touched the heart of Him. He didn't question her past, her profession, nor did He dismiss her from His presence. Her response to Him is what He desires in all believers. Jesus was looking at her heart. He honored her with these words, "her many sins have been forgiven – for she loved much. But he who has been forgiven little loves little." (John 7:47)

She had an opportunity to change her life, and she took advantage of it at all cost. We must pray and thank God for His power to overcome our sins and to demonstrate His victory over sin's power. When we come with a sacrificial offering of love and devotion, God will receive us into His Kingdom. Jesus will forgive us of all of our sins, and the Holy Spirit will fill us and empower us to carry out the will of God. Remember, God uses ordinary people to change the life of ordinary people.

God uses our suffering as a catalyst for our spiritual growth and change. Knowing that we must suffer and that our suffering is for our perfecting, divine purpose, and preservation, here are some tips to help us:

- Identify the specific reason for your suffering, and then follow the appropriate response, according to the word of God.

- Believe that God cares for you deeply, regardless of how severe your circumstances are. See (Rom. 8:36). Suffering should never lead you to deny God's love for you or to reject Him as your Lord and Savior

- Turn to God in earnest prayer and seek His face. Wait for Him until He delivers you from your afflictions (Psalms 130).

- Expect God to give you the grace necessary to bear your affliction, until deliverance comes (2 Corinthians 12:7-10). Always remember, "we are more than conquerors."

- Read the word of God, especially those Psalms that give comfort in times of affliction (Psalms 121).

- Seek revelation and discernment from God regarding your situation – through prayer, scripture and the enlightenment of the Holy Spirit or the counsel of a mature, godly believer.

- Remember, as believers we will all endure adversity, but God has promised to deliver us out of them all.

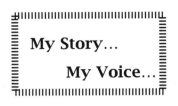

My Story...

My Voice...

Jesus was made perfect in His suffering. Therefore, we too are made perfect in our suffering! Being made perfect in my suffering was a hard lesson for me to learn.

When I used to commute to work, the first scripture I committed to memory was, "And not only so, but we glory in tribulations also: knowing that tribulation worketh patience; and patience, experience; and experience, hope." (Romans 5:3-4) Every day I had an hour train ride and a ten-minute walk from the Long Island Railroad to my office. It gave me the opportunity to study the word of God in peace. There was no husband, no children, and no responsibilities; just me and God. The walk to the office was my time to talk to God about everything concerning me and this scripture was being embedded in my spirit and my heart!

Yes, I was facing great tribulations, and I was seeking God for a way to escape. I continually wrestled with this whole idea that "we glory in tribulations." I cried out to the Lord for answers to my problems, and He kept telling me, "we glory in tribulations!" Imagine my despair! With everything that I was going through, the Holy Spirit was telling me there was glory in it! My mother was critically ill, and my marriage was dying. I was juggling being a mother of three while commuting an hour to and from work. I was also actively engaged in the church's ministry and believed that there was a ministry living in me. So, how do you find glory when it looks like everything is falling apart?

Here's what I learned: when I am empty, He fills my cup. The Lord is a cup filler, and He will let it overflow. In the midst of my brokenness, I decided to let Him in. His cup-filling ability has the power to strengthen you. He gave me the strength and ability to believe that I was more than a conqueror! The more I trusted God, the more He trusted me. My patience brought me my deliverance. It opened the door for my release. I was freed from my pity-party, and it released me to "stand fast in Christ!" (Galatians 5:1) This freedom gave me hope for my tomorrow! Now I know that having hope has a spiritual expectation.

Although I have been criticized, scandalized, persecuted, and rejected, I still had my voice! My voice, driven by the Holy Spirit, was like Jeremiah, who cried out that His word is like fire in my bones! The revelation of Romans 5:3-4, became real to me. There was glory in my tribulations, and it was working for my good. "Out of my brokenness, His glory is revealed." While others were looking at my burdens, my problems, setbacks and situations, God's glory was permeating my spirit to its spiritual perfection. I now had hope to endure!

Where Do We Go From Here?

By now you should have experienced the journey from having a spirit of unbelief to restored faith, to confessing with your mouth and believing with our heart. We now know that our faith is our substance, and we understand that our suffering has a purpose that perfects and preserves our relationship with Christ.

Is there a leaping in your spirit with excitement? Knowing that God the Father and Creator, Jesus the Son and Mediator and the Holy Spirit, Comforter and Guide are working within in our lives to bring us to a better state. I believe God that your life is being changed and that you are ready to shift to the place that He has for you. It's time to take action. There remains the challenge to build our spiritual confidence, spiritual courage and spiritual compassion. Since we cannot forget the warnings previously presented, (the danger of neglect, the danger of unbelief, the danger of not maturing and the danger of falling away), we must move forward!

So, where do we go from here?

If we are willing to take heed of the warnings in the book of Hebrews, we should also be as willing to receive the "Words of Exhortation," found here as well. Each exhortation begins with the phrase, "Let us...." I believe this is a call for action and response to the warnings stated above. I've found in the Word of God that, whenever there is a rebuke, an exhortation will follow. God is so sovereign in His dealings with us that He doesn't just reprimand, but also gives us a way out. An exhortation is a word of encouragement, comfort, or an appeal. It also speaks seriously, to prevent an action or bring a certain action to an end. It brings truth to light. It is also a motivation to live God's way (Acts 14:22). Here, the exhorter is operating with the goal of guiding us to obedience to God and His word.

The exhortations, found in Hebrews, are calling us out of our spiritual comfort zones. It's calling us to go higher. It's time to move from wherever we are right now to the next step. Understand, everyone is in a different place or a different plateau. It doesn't matter what step you are on; it's time to move up to the next step. Don't look back, because you don't want to remain trapped in your past, but freed from being bound! Whatever God is calling or bringing you to, He will supply every one of your needs for this season. Trusting Him is the key to your victory. You've got to take this step by faith! We are moving beyond our circumstances and situations, beyond our doubts and fears, and beyond what we can see or even think! God's word is true, and it will accomplish what it is set out to do. Therefore these exhortations, taken from the word of God, are true, and they will accomplish in you what God has assigned for it to do.

Please repeat this prayer:

Father, in the name of Jesus, I commit myself to a sanctified (set apart) life of holiness, and to please You. Your Word says to wash ourselves and make us clean; to cease to do evil and learn to do well. Therefore, Father, I repent and turn from any sin in my life. Wash me with the water of Your Word. I'm cleansed from all filthiness of the flesh and spirit, perfecting holiness in fear and reverence of You, Lord.

Father, I receive Your forgiveness now and thank You for it because Your Word says You are faithful and just to forgive us our sins and to cleanse us from all unrighteousness. Thank You for your Son, who brings wisdom, righteousness, sanctification, and redemption.

I submit myself to You, Lord – spirit, soul and body. I commit to change whatever needs to change in my life. The desire of my heart is to be a vessel unto honor, sanctified and fitting for the Master's use and prepared for every good work. In Jesus name, Amen.

The 1ˢᵗ exhortation

I want to pour this into your spirit, "Let us come boldly before the throne of grace, that we may obtain mercy and find grace to help in time of need." (Hebrews 4:16) Each exhortation begins with "let us," which is calling for the body of Christ to make a collective or group effort to move to action. There's a circle of people already assigned to your life (whether family, friends, co-workers or other believers) as a group. Know that you are not the only one who needs to move; moreover, you are not the only one taking this step right now! The "let us," is a reminder of our link to the body of Christ, and we are all being encouraged as a group to move forward. We are moving by faith and not by sight, but we must be in one accord, with one another for the benefit of the "let us!" The "let us," is the church today, and we need to move into action!

This exhortation is calling for us to come!

- To come means to believe (Acts 16:31)
- To receive (John 1:12)
- To eat (John 6:35)
- To drink (John 7:37)
- To look (Isa. 45:22)

- To confess (1 John 4:2)

- To hear (John 5:24)

- To enter a door (John 10:9)

- To open a door (Revelation 3:20)

- To touch the hem of His garment (Matthew 9:20-21)

- To accept the gift of eternal life through Christ our Lord (Romans 6:23)

- And to come to Me (Matthew 11:28).

This usage of the word, "come" is a gracious invitation from Christ, who is ready, willing and able to meet every need and answer every prayer. It's a call to all "who are weary and burdened" with the troubles of this world and the sins of our lives. By coming to Jesus, you become submissive to becoming His servant and obeying His direction. He will free you from your insurmountable burdens and give you rest. His Holy Spirit will lead you through this spiritual life. Whatever trials and cares you carry, you will endure with His help and grace.

Because we have a great High Priest, who sympathizes with our weaknesses, we should be encouraged to come actively or move in response to His appeal to us. Not only does the Word suggest for us to come, but we are to come boldly! *BOLDLY* is the posture we need to be in when we come to our Savior and King. It also means to come near without hesitation or fear and to draw closer with confidence. Our confidence is based on the knowledge that He died to save us and that He lives to keep us. It is a by-product of our faith and love for God that we're convinced that He is there for us in every area of our lives. As we possess this trait, we become more willing to come boldly. Because He is the great High Priest, he can sympathize with us because of His suffering experiences. When we come boldly to the throne of grace, He is waiting for us with His infinite wisdom and power. We have the spiritual confidence to approach the heavenly throne because our prayers and petitions are welcomed. Proverbs 3:26 says, "For the Lord will be your confidence, and He will keep your foot from being snared." The Lord guards those who walk in His ways. He won't let your foot get caught in a trap.

Jesus is a great resource for His people. He has passed through the heavens (beyond the atmosphere and stellar) and is equal with God; He is the Great High Priest. "Therefore, do not cast away your confidence, which has great reward." (Hebrews 10:36) Let us come!

The 2ⁿᵈ exhortation

I want to impart this, "Let us hold fast the confession of our hope without wavering, for He who promised is faithful." (Hebrews 10:23) This exhortation may appear to be simple. However, it is potent. The action we are being called to is, to hold fast! Before you begin thinking that this is easy to do, let me remind you of the Israelites and how many times they failed to hold fast to God. Throughout the Old Testament, we hear their stories of disobedience which resulted in captivity. "Although they knew God, they did not glorify Him as God, nor were they thankful, but became futile in their thoughts, and their foolish hearts were darkened." (Romans 1:21) They "exchanged the truth of God for the lie, and worshiped and served the creature rather than the Creator, who is blessed forever, Amen." (Romans 1:24) They did the opposite of holding fast; they let go of their faith and their hope!

To hold means to have or keep in the hand; to grasp; to hold something in place. In the book of Revelations, we find Jesus encouraging the churches to hold fast! When John writes to the church in Thyatira, they're applauded for their deeds, love, and faith. They were doing more than they did at first. However, they tolerated Jezebel. She called herself a prophet, misleading them into sexual immorality and into eating food sacrificed to idols. The church in Thyatira had the tendency of tolerating sin and unrighteousness. In other words, because the people were comfortable with the prevalent sins they opened the door of their heart to a sinful spirit. Christ declared His punishment to Jezebel and then He addresses the church. "Now I say to the rest of you in Thyatira, to you who do not hold to her teaching and have not learned Satan's so-called deep secrets, I will put no other burden on you. Only hold on to what you have until I come." (Revelation 2:24-25) The rest of you refers to those who were willing and had the spiritual courage to hold to Christ's word and His promises. This remnant didn't succumb to the temptations of Jezebel's teaching. Jezebel used treachery and murdered to get her way. She was a wicked woman who led the Israelites deeper into idolatry. They lacked the spiritual courage to dismiss the spirit of Jezebel. To have spiritual courage means to be in the state or quality of mind that enables one to face danger with spiritual authority. To be spiritual is to have a holy frame of mind. It's an ideal state of the word dwelling richly in you. Not being conceited, provoking or envying one another. The author is calling the true believer to hold fast, with spiritual confidence and courage, to resist the enemy's attempts to lure you into spiritual immorality and being a spiritual murderer or to commit spiritual suicide. He wants us to be courageous while we wait for Him.

To the church of Philadelphia, he writes, "What doors He opens, no one can shut, and what doors He shuts, no one can open. I know your deeds. See, I have placed before you an open door that no one can shut. I know that you have little strength, yet you have kept my word and have not denied my name." (Revelation 3:7-8) Philadelphia was a faithful church that kept God's word and did not deny Him. They had endured opposition from the world and resisted conforming to the evil trends. They had preserved in their loyalty to Christ. They faced their dangers with spiritual courage. Because of their per-severing, God promised to deliver them from the hour of trial. The hour of trial is to the Great Tribulation, the wrath of God, in the end, times. He further encourages them in verse 11, "I am coming soon. Hold on to what you have so that that no-one will take your crown." The church is encouraged to hold on to Christ and His Word. What a great blessing we have in Christ. He has prepared a crown for us. He is convinced that we will arrive in His heavenly kingdom. All we have to do is just, hold fast!

We are exhorted to hold on to what we have or what we have confessed to believing. Whether you are a member of Thyatira or Philadelphia, promises have been made to rescue you from the hand of the enemy if you hold fast. Holding on to our confession is essential to maintaining our relationship with Christ Jesus. Hebrews 3:6, says, "But Christ is faithful as a son over God's house. And we are His house if we hold on to our courage and the hope of which we boast." Our spiritual security is maintained as we cooperate with God's grace by persevering in faith and holiness to the end! We can't give up, and we can't let go! We have to go on to our perfection in Christ Jesus.

This exhortation says to "hold fast the confession of our hope without wavering." When we confess, we are openly admitting our personal wrongdoings. However, this confession is to declare or acknowledge Jesus as Lord; for He is the rock we must stand on. Remember Jesus' conversation with Peter, when He asked, "Whom do you say that I am?" Peter answered, "You are the Christ!" Jesus responded, "Flesh and blood have not revealed this to you, but My Father, who is in heaven. And I say to you Peter, "That on this rock I will build my church, and the gates of Hades shall not prevail against it." (Matt. 16:13-18) We are to hold on to this same hope that Jesus gave to Peter. Christ says that He is building His church in us and that the gates of Hades will not prevail against us. Paul also advises "we can no longer be children, tossed to and fro by the wave; blown here and there by every wind of teaching; and by the cunning and craftiness of men in their deceitful scheming." (Eph. 4:14) We must be spiritually mature in our Christian walk and filled with the fullness of Christ. We must also become mature and be able to discern the things of God. Infants are immature, unstable and easily deceived by false doctrine. We, who are growing in God, should hold on to the truth of the gospel, present it in love and resist demonic spirits.

The 3<u>rd</u> exhortation

I want to deposit in you, "Let us lay aside every weight and the sin that so easily ensnares (besets) us and let us run with endurance the race that is set before us." (Hebrews 12:1) The author is informing his audience that their current situation is no different from any of the sufferings of those that went before them. He refers to them as those, "now surrounding us as a great cloud of witnesses." (Hebrews 12:1) They are witnessing to us by their lives of faith and endurance and have set a great precedent for us to duplicate.

Through their testimony, we hear the clarion call from the author to, "lay aside the weight!" In ministry, I've learned that too many of us are carrying our burdens around where ever we go! We'll hear the altar call to bring our burdens to the Lord and leave them there. But, we are so attached to our issues that we can't seem to separate ourselves from them. God is trying to free us from the bondage, but we won't let go! We continue to live in the past, repeating the story, and holding onto the weight! In an episode of "Oprah's Master Class," I heard Iyanla Vanzant addressing an audience participant. He began telling his story of being a recovering addict. In the midst of his storytelling, Iyanla stopped him and said, "Stop telling your get high story. Every time you tell your get high story, it's another time for you to get high. Each time you tell it, you're reliving it, and it's like you're shooting up again!"

Some of us are like the participator. Are you getting high with your story of hurts, disappointments, or setbacks? There is a place and a time for you to tell your story. But, if the story you have been telling is holding you hostage to your past, then it's time to move on. We can be our worst enemy by allowing the emotional attachments to cripple us. Once I realized that my memories, stories, hurt, and pain were weighing me down, I had to make the choice to free myself from the weight. I had to begin peeling off the layers of despair to get free. I realized that I kept piling this and that into my suitcase of life. Stuff that didn't belong to me, that others had afflicted, and the stuff that I wasn't willing to face and conquer. It's like our physical diets when we don't pay attention to what we eat, how we feed ourselves continually and not partake in exercise, we become grossly overweight. Yes, it happened to me, and I didn't see it coming. I had to change my eating habits and incorporate physical exercise into my daily routine.

The Holy Spirit revealed to me that there is a sin attached to every weight (heaviness, load, or burden) we carry. What do I mean? This type of sin is called "a besetting sin." According to Elmer L. Towns, author of "Fasting for Spiritual Breakthrough," besetting sins make you a slave and take away your will to overcome. Besetting sins are habitual sinful behaviors or attitudes that victimize and enslave (beset) people. For example, the weight of alcoholism is connected to the sin of overindulging or drinking too much (gluttony). The weight of bitterness connects to the sin of unforgiveness (wrath). The weight of fornication connects to the sin of adultery (lust).

Ordinary "willpower" cannot break the yoke of besetting sin because we are chained to it like a compulsive addict. The question is, "Are you in bondage?" "Have you allowed yourself to be brought into captivity?" If the answer is yes, "How do you get free?"

Bondage comes when we believe Satan's lies to us about sin instead of God's truth. He gets us to believe one of the following:

- ✓ I tried before, and I can't break it.

- ✓ I don't want to do this, but I can't help it.

- ✓ I need an answer (now), but I can't find it.

Although we can change our desires, and find the answers, we believe we are powerless because we have surrendered our wills to Satan rather than to God. When Satan controls our thoughts, he controls our lives. When he lies to us about our lives, and we believe it, we are in bondage!

The Power of the Disciple's Fast

Bondage can be broken the same way Jesus did during His ministry. When Jesus dealt with the demonized boy, He said this problem was so severe, ordinary means could not break him. "This kind goeth not out but by prayer and fasting." (Matthew 17:21) Breaking free from bondage requires a different action than what you are probably used to. Jesus not only wanted to help the demonized boy, but He also wanted to teach His disciples how to dig deeper. He needs us to take our focus off of the problem and focus on His solution. His word of encouragement to overcome the demonic spirit is by prayer and fasting. If we've obeyed the call to come boldly to the throne of grace, we must now surrender our will to His will, by fasting.

The Disciple's Fast is a tool that has helped me to gain control in my life. When I read, "Fasting for Spiritual Breakthrough," Townsend, I learned, "The purpose of all worship, including fasting, is to change the worshipper in ways that have a social and personal impact. We worship not to just gratify ourselves, but also to become empowered to change the world! I had this book for several years, and I routinely practiced the St. Paul's, Daniel's and the John the Baptist fast. Each fast were effective at their appointed time; however, once the Lord led me to begin a Discipleship Ministry, I was in awe to learn that there was a Disciple's Fast for breaking bondage. "A significant reason to fast is to release people from the bondage of sin." Townsend's resolve is, "When you take control of your physical appetite, you develop the strength to take control of your emotional appetite." If you are wrestling with control of your life, you can find refuge in this fast. By controlling what you eat, you determine that you will control your life for God's purpose. You move into the strength of decision-making. You strengthen yourself to stand against a force that has enslaved your spiritual appetite."

Do you want to be made well? When Jesus asked the crippled man this question, He was arousing the willpower of the crippled man. Jesus wanted the man to desire the "power" that He could give him. He wants us to look within to make the decision to follow Him. "He wants you to have a "faith-experience" (recognize what God can do); which will lead to a "faith-expression" (speaking of what God can do); to a "faith event" (fasting for spiritual breakthrough)."

To break spiritual bondage, we must follow the steps God has provided for this spiritual warfare:

"For the weapons of our warfare are not carnal, but mighty through God to the pulling down of strong holds; casting down imaginations and every high thing that exalts itself against the knowledge of God, and bringing into captivity every thought to the obedience of Christ." (2 Corinthians 10:4-5)

Step 1: Renounce Counterfeit Control – we must discern reality from counterfeit. Anything that controls your mind that is not from Christ is counterfeit (Romans 12:2).

Step 2: Acknowledge Self-Deception – it involves acknowledging our efforts to deceive ourselves and choosing to embrace the truth of God. We deceive ourselves when we think we can sin and escape the consequences (1 Corinthians 6:9).

Step 3: Forgive to Overcome Bitterness – we need to forgive others so we can overcome bitterness and gain freedom. When you refuse to forgive (for whatever reason), you place yourself in spiritual bondage to them and to sin (2 Corinthians 2:10-11).

Step 4: Submit to God's Authority – overcoming the rebellion in your life by submitting to the authority of God and those He has placed over you. We have to deal with our rebellious spirit and attitude.

Step 5: Take Personal Responsibility - confront the problem of pride with a spirit of humility. You are called upon to renounce and repent every sin in your body, and not just say I'm sorry. When you humble yourself before God, you enable Him to bless you with the freedom He desires to give you.

Step 6: Disown Sinful Influences – this involves disowning sinful influences that come from friends and acquaintances. You will need the power of the Holy Spirit and continual prayer to complete this step.

Once you complete this process, you will be equipped to run this Christian race with endurance. Freeing yourself from the weight and the sin allows you to become disciplined to run. Therefore, "Let us run with endurance the race that's set before us." (Hebrews 12:1) Our ability to endure is at stake. We have to stay the course, remain in Christ, and be firm in our faith. Think about the athlete or the many that train to run marathons. They have to train, eat properly, and get sufficient rest to stay focused in all their efforts just to run the race. As we run, our eyes must be fixed, and our hearts set on Jesus Christ. We have to look to Jesus, who is the author and finisher of our faith. We each have our personal race to run. If we endure to the end, we will receive the joy and reward of completing the race that He has set before us.

When I think about running a race with endurance, I immediately think of the NBA and the NFL. Each association has to train their teams in preparation for the season. The NBA regular season starts in either late October or early November. Every team plays 82 regular season games. The playoffs usually start in mid-April and conclude with the NBA Finals in early-to-mid June. A normal NFL season begins late August or early September and ends in late December or early January. Every NFL team plays 16 regular season games. The playoffs take place during the month of January and concludes with the Super Bowl, on the first Sunday of February. With both sports being physically challenging, we know that the teams must train and prepare for their seasons. I believe that the training is intense and a rigorous workout. This type of workout and preparation is something the average person probably could not endure. Not me for sure! If the players are not physically fit for the training, they will not survive the season.

I learned that during their training seasons, the team members are brought together to reconnect with the administration and their fellow team members, to form a cohesiveness that will facilitate the team being on one accord. They have to learn each other's abilities and weaknesses to effectively support one another and develop their strategies to win the season.

Each of us belongs to the Kingdom of God. We are on His team, and He is the owner of the team. He is refining us and preparing us to win the battles. He knows that we have to be equipped to endure hardships, persecutions, trials and tribulations, rejections, wrath, and the temptation. He knows that without His discipline, we would not be able to endure the race set before us. He wants us to bear witness to His power, presence and purpose, in our lives to others. Like the great crowd of witnesses (mentioned in Hebrews 11), we must overcome by faith. We also have to be trained, by the Holy Spirit, to utilize the weapons of our warfare and not the weapons of this world. We don't have the burden of winning the games and making it to the play-offs, but we are to win souls to Christ with our testimony. Many are on the sidelines of our life, watching how we engage. They want to see if we're disciplined in the power of Christ. Are you fit to run this race and are you able to endure to the end? Laying aside the weight and preparing ourselves to run this race, in Christ, will win the race and He will give us the VICTORY!

My Story...
My Voice...

"O house of Israel, can I not do with you as this potter does?" declares the Lord. "Like clay in the hand of the potter, so are you in my hand, O house of Israel." (Jeremiah 18:6)

God's plans are not our plans, His thoughts, are not our thoughts and His ways are not our ways (Isaiah 55:8, Paraphrased). Because I knew there was still a place, in God that I had to get to, I knew I still had to surrender more of myself to His will. "Can I not do with you as the potter does with the clay?" How many times did I ponder, "What else, and where else was He going to take me before I would arrive?" I continued to be obedient to teaching, preaching, ministering and interceding, as the Holy Spirit instructed. The favor of the Lord was upon me, and He was allowing my gifts to be manifested before men. The more I did what He told me to do; the more effective and strengthened the ministry became. Being strengthened encouraged me to believe that my divine purpose was at hand and in due season, I would walk into my destiny.

A few years ago during one of our Women's Day weekend celebration, Friday night service, the preacher challenged us to get up and pursue what the Lord has prepared for us. *She told us that we were waiting for the bus, but the bus wasn't coming. Growing up in Brooklyn, NY, I immediately identified with the analogy of waiting for the bus. I thought about the many times; I waited for a bus that was either late, too full or just wasn't coming! I would be still, sitting and waiting. Because I connected with the preacher's vision, I was immediately and spiritually challenged to move from the bus stop. I knew it was time to find other means of transportation to my God-ordained destination. Sitting at the bus stop meant I was relying on other people to get me to where I needed, and I was not considering my options. Again, I heard the Lord say, "Can I not do to you what the potter does with the clay?" Finally, I said yes Lord, you can do to me what the potter does to the clay!*

Hallelujah, I'm not at the bus stop, I am moving towards my divine destiny, and I am allowing God, through the power of His Holy Spirit to lead and guide me to that place. The Holy Spirit had given me glimpses of what I looked like operating within my purpose, but I still had to get there. Not according to my will, I had to let His will be done. Now, I've leaped off the bench, shook off the bus stop clothes, put a pep in my step, and I'm ready for the journey.

God was speaking! Daughter, there are still some things that I have to take you through to prepare you for the place that I have ordained. I have to equip you; therefore, you must be put on the potter's wheel, to be formed. After the wheel, I will place you in the oven for baking. You must be still in the oven, to set the mold for where you will be. Then, I will put you in the fiery furnace, to burn off any imperfections I see! He said I want to use you "as my servant and a witness of what you have seen of me and what I will show you." (Acts 26:16) So you must endure this process.

There is always a process that we must endure. The process breaks us from our soul ties and restores us as new creatures in Christ. Our old ways are cast away and behold; we are made brand new." (1 Corinthians 5:17) The journey was beyond my spiritual capacity, beyond my understanding, and beyond my doubts and fears. Hearing the Holy Spirit was more than enough for me to believe beyond the journey.

Leaving the bus stop meant I could no longer rely on the worldly or carnal transportation. I was moving by the power of the Holy Spirit. I had to let go of situations, forgive the unforgivable, and hold on to God's unchanging hand. He told me that He was using me because I trusted in Him. It was by faith, I met Him, by faith, I trusted Him and by faith, I was following Him.

I thought the world around me was changing; no, it was the Spirit that dwelled deeper on the inside that was changing me. Now, I had the faith to reach the unreachable, to fight the unbeatable, with faith that stands the invincible and faith that can conquer anything.

You Don't Have to See it To Believe It!

"Behold (see, pay attention, be alert, or wit-ness), I will do a new thing; now it shall spring forth: shall ye not perceive it? I will even make a way in the wilderness and rivers in the desert." (Isaiah 43:19)

Whenever you hear the Word of the Lord saying, "Behold," it's time to stop and pay attention to what is about to happen. When I've come across this word biblically, I've noticed that it is an indication that something supernatural is about to happen. Since we've come to the end (or maybe the beginning for some) of this journey, I want you to know that something supernatural is about to happen. It's supernatural because it is above and beyond what is natural; it is un-explainable and could be considered a phe-nomena! Yes, the time is now for you to walk into your destiny, your divine purpose, your God-ordained vision. Prophet Isaiah declared a word of encouragement to the children of Israel, after his word of rebuke. (Remember, where there is a rebuke, there's always an ex-hortation.) Isaiah is exhorting the people of God to pay attention, be alert to what he is about to declare to them, from the Lord!

He told the people to, "Forget the for-mer things, and do not dwell on the things of old (vs. 18)!" Do not hold on to the things that you have been through, to forget about who has hurt you, rejected you, disappointed you, neglected you or even abused you. He says, don't dwell on those things. Those are the former things, and those things are considered old! It's over! If you don't let the former and the old things go now, they will continue to have authority over you, and you will remain in bondage, for the next seven years! The hour of visitation is here! It's time for you to be set free by the Power of the Holy Spirit. Don't be like Lot's wife, when the angel's arrived to save them from the destruction of Sodom and Gomorrah! The angels said to Lot, "Do you have anyone else here – sons-in-law, sons or daughters, or anyone else in the city who belongs to you? Get them out of here, because we are going to destroy this place (Genesis 19:12-13). They further urged him, saying, "Take your wife and your two daughters who are here, or you will be swept away when the city is punished." (vs. 15) Lot's wife looked back, and she became a pillar of salt (vs. 26). You can't afford to look back at the former things! You have to sanctify (separate) yourself from those things and draw nigh to God. Before you perish with them, He's calling you to come out from among them.

Sodom and Gomorrah are symbols of wickedness and destruction. However, Lot's family was the only ones spared. Your life is being spared if you obey the voice of the Lord and forget the former things; do not dwell on the things of old and get out of the city of your past. If you look back, again, you will be struck down or become spiritually dead! The theory for Lot's wife is that her heart was clinging to the pleasures of Sodom and Gomorrah. One could also argue it was possible she was clinging to her earthly treasures she had acquired from living in the city. Maybe she didn't believe that the city was being destroyed. Whatever she was clinging to, it cost her, her life!

In spite of our unfaithfulness, our doubts, and fears, our weaknesses, and insecurities, God still has the plan to deliver us from evil. He still wants to show us His tender mercies, morning by morning. He is still performing miracles, signs and wonders to demonstrate His loving-kindness, wisdom, and power. He does all of this, "that we might believe." (John 20:31)

"I will do a new thing!" God has promised to change the life of His children. It's going to be different from what we've experienced, different from what we're familiar with, different from anything we have ever seen before! It's going to be new. "Therefore, if any man be in Christ, he is a new creature; the old things are passed away and behold, all things become new." (2 Corinthians 5:17) The new is within you. You have to believe God is doing a work in you, and your life is changing. The beauty of being born-again is that we get the opportunity of a second chance, a do-over! God wants to change our heart and our mind, to be not conformed to this world, but to be transformed by the "renewing" of our mind." (Romans 12:2) What's so phenomenal is that His word has the power to change your spirit, which will change your thinking and your behavior. The Holy Spirit's presence in you is the manifestation of His power changing you. Add your faith to the Word, presence and power of God to experience the fullness of your transformation. Don't resist it because it's new and unfamiliar. God is answering your silent prayers. He knows precisely what you need, and when you need it. Remember, He knows the exact combination of pressure and high temperature to cause the formation of diamond crystals. Everything that you have gone through has been part of your divine formation process, to bring you forth as the diamond He has ordained you to be! The quality of these diamond crystals cannot be purchased or manufactured by man; it is only by the power of the Most High God!

It's a new thing that is coming forth! Isaiah asked the people of God, shall you not perceive it? This question is not a tricky one, but a thought-provoking one. We think, if we can't see it, it's not happening! Nothing can be further from the truth! He specifically asked, shall you not perceive it? Seeing it means that it's something tangible. Moreover, we think if we see it, then we can believe it. Well, the prophet asked if we "shall not perceive it?" What's the difference? To perceive means that you have come to understand, recognize, discern or envision something. It's the way you think about it; having the ability to understand. In other words, it's a knowing in your spirit, not something carnal or seen. So again, "it's coming forth: shall you not perceive it?

He didn't ask if you can see it because this is not about what you can see. You should be able to close your eyes and still be able to see or perceive that which is coming forth. The Holy Spirit is at work in you too:

- ✓ Recall the things of God
- ✓ Recall your first love connection with Him
- ✓ Recall the grace that He has given to you to repent
- ✓ Recall the purpose of your restoration
- ✓ Recall His power that He has deposited in you

If you can perceive it, then you can receive it! Don't be deceived by the evil spirit. He wants you to stay stuck in limbo, stuck in bondage and stuck in the pit! He wants you to believe that if you can't see it, then you can't believe. That you are blind, and you will never receive your sight! But God!

"God so loved the world that He gave His only begotten Son; that whosoever believes in Him, shall not perish but have everlasting." (John 3:16) God loves us so much that He sacrificed His Son for our sake. He set the stage for us to walk into our spiritual destiny, from where we are! However, the condition was not that we see it, but that we believe it! It's another supernatural experience. Watch this, He says, if you "believe in Him (Jesus), you will not perish. To perish means that you will die due to harsh conditions. But Jesus is telling us that if we "believe" on Him, we will not perish. By faith, we receive life in Christ and the promise that we will not perish. Take a moment to think and reflect on all the things, you've been delivered from! Think about the things that you know God has forgiven. You are freed from the bondage of sin! So, no matter what it "looks" like you are going through, you have to perceive the promise that you will not perish. Instead, you shall have everlasting life! He is referring to a spiritual death, not the physical death. Your spiritual life will not perish; it will live.

This might seem to be unexplainable, (because it's something that you can't see). Eternal life changes the quality of your life. You are not living without hope; you are now living with the joy of the Lord. You are no longer living in darkness; you are now living in the marvelous light. You are no longer living in doubt and fear; you are now living by faith. You are no longer living in chaos and confusion; you are living in the peace of God which surpasses all understanding! What a phenomena!

I pray that you are no longer waiting to see it, but believe it beyond your wildest imagination. Mary, the mother of Jesus, couldn't believe that she would bear a child since she did not know a man (Luke 1:26-34). The disciples didn't believe the multitude could be fed with two fish and five loaves of bread. Martha and Mary didn't believe their brother Lazarus could be raised from the dead. Their faith was challenged to a new height. The door of their faith was opened to believe in Jesus Christ and the power of His word.

You see, Mary, the disciples, and Martha and Mary were used to bring a change to the world by the power of the Holy Spirit. He's changing your life now so that you will be able to bring change to someone's life. Can you perceive that the POWER is at work within you to completely accomplish infinitely more! He's completing the work that He has begun in you; however, we need to invest in what God is doing, on your behalf. The Prophet Isaiah says the Lord declares, "I will even make a way in the wilderness and rivers in the desert." (Isaiah 43:19) He will make a road through the desert for His people as they return from captivity. On the renewed earth, the waste places will enjoy plentiful water supplies so that the creatures of the wilderness will be grateful.

How many of us are or have been in a wilderness experience? Life sometimes seems like a wilderness experience with its ups and downs. Feelings of alienation and rejection rise and you are facing the fear of not surviving. The Israelites traveled throughout the wilderness to get to the promised land of Canaan. Their wilderness experience lasted for forty years, because of their disobedience and their sin! God set them free and just like them; He will deliver you too! He's making a path, just for you, in the wilderness. You've traveled this way before, but now a path is being made for you to make an exodus from sin, darkness, the past, your fears, and your unbelief. Remember, He opens doors that no man can shut!

God's not only making a path for your exodus; He is also sending you refreshing water to quench your thirst in the desert. He is sending rivers of water to restore your faith and restore your quest for life. You can live again, even after you've been in the wilderness or the desert all of this time. Your wilderness experiences are the former things, and the river is cleansing you from all unrighteousness. It's resuscitating you from the choke-holds of life. "Whoever drinks of this water will thirst again, but whoever drinks of the water that I shall give him will never thirst. But the water that I shall give him will become in him a fountain of water springing up into everlasting life! (John 4:13-14) Whoever drinks of Christ's blessings and mercies will never thirst again. Not only does His benefits fill the heart, but it overflows it as well.

This message is universal, for the universal body of Christ. "Behold!" He is doing a new thing in all who will seek after Him. He also promises a great reward to those who will overcome! The way has been paved to come out of the wilderness and be restored with refreshing water. Christ says, if you have an ear, then hear (perceive that which is coming and receive it as a state of being) what the Spirit is saying for you to do. As the Lord spoke to His servant John, the Word of the Lord is still speaking to us today in "The Revelations." John writes to the seven churches bearing witness to "the things that are," perceived by Jesus the Christ. The churches (the true believers) are being called out of their former things and exhorted to operate in the things of God! Every church is being called, individually, to overcome.

At first, I thought I was supposed to share with you the seven different promises the Lord makes to them that overcomes. But what the Holy Spirit has revealed is that the principle is in you heeding the warning to change as opposed to the benefit that you will receive. There are lessons for us to learn when we hear what the Spirit is saying to the church rather focusing on the benefits that we will receive. God's word is true, and it will accomplish what it is set out to do, so the burden is upon us to do what He is calling us to do. Jesus revealed it to John, and John reveals it to us; although revealed, we must perceive it and not just see it. If we rely on what we think we see, we will be deceived by our thoughts regarding the necessary actions and responses required. Everyone expects to see miracles, signs, and wonders; however, they only come forth to persuade the believer of the Power, Presence and Purpose of the ministry of Jesus the Christ. Miracles were and are His supernatural power. Signs are shown to signify spiritual truths and wonders are intended to arouse the amazement in the spectators. But, it does not exempt us from the action required by us!

He that hath an ear, let him hear what the Spirit is saying to the church!

My Story...

My Voice...

I didn't see it coming, but I still had to believe God beyond it.

I had been going through some health issues and was passive-aggressively addressing them. On a routine check-up, I was referred for my annual mammogram. I received a letter from the imaging laboratory that I needed to return for a follow-up! They saw something, but wanted to make sure it was nothing! I returned for the follow-up and had to have a biopsy! The results of the biopsy said, I had Breast Cancer!

I didn't see it coming, but I still had to believe God beyond it!

Before I knew it, I was sitting in front of a breast surgeon who was explaining my options. My head was spinning! Me, having to endure any surgery was beyond my mental, emotional and physical capacity! And the journey began.

I sought the Lord, asking, "God, are you going to stop me now?" I had finally arrived in ministry, the vision that He had given to me was manifesting, and I'm too busy for this distraction. Well, when I asked the question, I didn't hear an answer. I called a friend that *evening who had just buried her mom! She said she didn't understand why God allowed this to happen now. I replied, "God's timing is impeccable!" In her torn voice, she said, "it is such a dark place." I replied, "Only God understands the dark place." To my surprise, by ministering to my friend, I received the answers that I needed. I didn't see it coming, nor did I understand what was about to happen, but I knew, that His timing was impeccable, and only He understands my dark place.*

My family and friends were alarmed because everyone knew how petrified I am about hospitals, doctors, needles, and, etc. We were all amazed that I was facing this battle! I can't tell you that I wasn't afraid; however, I put all of my faith in God. I knew that what I had to go through was only more of my perfecting. The victory was mine! I knew that I would live and not die! The Holy Spirit comforted me with the peace of God that surpasses all understanding. Especially mine!

Here's what I knew for sure. There were people assigned to my life that needed to bear witness to my journey to encourage them in their faith. There was a fear in me that had to be released to reach those that He needed me to reach. I rejoiced in the Lord for the great things that He has done. This battle challenged my entire family and me!

I chose to have a mastectomy and breast reconstruction. The surgery lasted for nine and half hours. I could not imagine being sedated for that long. However, I heard the Spirit of the Lord saying; there are some things I need to remove and some things I have to insert. He didn't need me in His way!

I also learned the difference between being in pain and healing. The pain was temporary. Within two weeks, I was not in any real pain from the surgery. However, healing was much more intense. My body let me know I was not the same. I had to be still and patient for the healing process.

I didn't see it coming, but I still had to believe God through it!

Six weeks after surgery, I began my chemotherapy. Now, I've heard people talk about chemotherapy, seen women on television and in magazines who were Breast Cancer survivors and knew a few women who had suffered from it! None of this prepared me for it! It felt like a monster was invading my body, and it snatched every fiber of my being. The four months of treatment were awful, yet empowering!

I didn't see it coming, but I still had to believe God in it!

The treatments would take my strength, but I would find the strength to rise again! In spite of what I was going through, I held on to the joy of the Lord. My faith was enriched by experiencing only what He can do in the dark *place. I had hope in God that I would make it through. My voice wasn't as strong as usual, but He still heard my cry. I still encouraged others to believe in Him. I would just say, "God is a wonder!"*

The blessing was that the ministry (Christian Uprise Thru Edification Discipleship Ministry), did not die. The fellowship rallied around me, supported me, encouraged, fed, and prayed for me. It was testing all of our faith! My extended church family (The Oil of Joy Ministries II, Inc.), labored in prayer and believed God for my deliverance. Fueled by the work of the ministries, I had to keep on fighting!

I didn't see it coming, but I had to believe God!

I spent nine months home, recuperating and healing! I reconnected with myself and the vision that the Lord had for me to do. I had to let go of the social me and take care of the essential me. "He makes us to lie down in the green pastures; He leads us beside the still waters, and He restores our souls. He guides us in the path of righteousness for His name sake." (Psalms 23:2-3) The quiet time lead me to write this book. The Holy Spirit gave me the vision, the ability and the time to write it!

If I could have seen it, I probably would have told me that I couldn't do it. But thanks be to God, that I didn't have to see it, just believe!

<u>Now Faith!</u>

"To everything, there is a season, a time for every purpose under heaven." (Eccleciastes 3:1)

Now brings us to a specific place in time. It's signifying something happening now or in the next moment.

Now, requires a course of action, with no further delay.

Now, presents us with the opportunity to ponder where we've been and where we're about to go!

Now that we are coming to the close of this experience, we must examine the NOW! There is an urgency in the now; it is calling forth an immediate response from you, the true believer.

Now, is also in response to the words shared, to what you have heard, and to what you believe the Holy Spirit is, urging you to do. The time of "now" is for you to set (get or make ready) your wings for your transition. This preparation is for the new idea of a "now faith is." It's a "now faith," because you will begin to operate in it, oppose to you operating in a spirit of unbelief! You will overcome your fears with your new foundation of faith. You're understanding that your faith is your substance, that your suffering has a greater purpose and that you don't have to see it, to believe it.

By now you should be enlightened to "Believe Beyond," any obstacles, setbacks, misfortunes, rejection and/or neglect in your life. The "now faith" is also a posture of change, because of the warnings and exhortations that have led us into our experience together. It is suggesting a change from one state to another or one condition to another.

So, let us pack up our bags, leave our worries behind and move to the new idea of "kingdom living by faith, as we walk in our God-ordained destiny.

Before we can look at the new idea, I believe it's necessary to look at the content of what has been presented to us, to perceive how we are being encouraged to change. The unknown author began his writings of Hebrews by reminding us that, Christ is better than the angels because they worshiped Him. He is better than Moses, for He created Him. He is better than the Aaronic priesthood, for His sacrifice was once and for all. He is better than the law, for He mediates a better covenant. In short, there is more to be gained in Christ than to become lost in tradition (or in the things of this world). He stresses that pressing on in Christ produces a tested faith, self-discipline, and visible love. The author also lets us know that Christ is our High Priest; the mediator and perfecter of our faith! He is superior to all who went before us and offered the supreme sacrifice, priesthood, and covenant!

Hebrews 4:14-16 says, "Seeing then that we have a great High Priest, who has passed through the heavens, Jesus, the Son of God, let us hold fast our confessions. For we do not have a High Priest, who cannot sympathize with our weaknesses, but was in all points tempted as we are, yet without sin. Let us, therefore, come boldly to the throne of grace that we may obtain mercy and find grace to help in our time of need!"

He wants us to see clearly that Jesus is the Great High Priest. In Judaism, the Aaronic priesthood would have to go to the tabernacle once a year to offer up sacrifices to atone for their sins and the sins of the people. First, the priest would have to cleanse himself, then offer atonement for the people. If the priest was not right in the sight of the Lord, he would not survive in the tabernacle and would have to be dragged out! With Jesus, as our High Priest, He made a once and for all sacrifice for us; moreover, He did not have to be cleaned or repent for His sins because He was without sin! There is no greater love and no greater sacrifice.

Because of His sacrifice and His divine power to overcome temptation, we "now" have a High Priest that can sympathize with our weaknesses! Thank God for His provisions. We are no longer subject to the penalty of sin or the shame. If we confess our sins, He will forgive our sin, and we will be free to live the abundant life. What a mighty God we serve. His love covers a multitude of sin and His spirit of love, longsuffering, and patience, is the drawing power that brings us back into the fold!

He may not answer your prayer the way that you want Him to, but He will answer your prayer the way you need Him to! You have to show up! Come boldly, with confidence. Your confidence has to be in your faith. You must be firmly convinced that God can do what He says He can do. Jesus, the Great High Priest, is already interceding on your behalf, and He will supply all of your needs, according to His riches in glory! We have to get to the throne of grace! The throne is considered a special place (a special chair), for a king, a powerful person. It is the position of the king, as one with royal power and authority. Grace is God's presence and love through Christ Jesus, given to believers by the Holy Spirit. His grace sets us free from sin and gives us the ability to act according to His will. Faith gives us a place to stand; Grace gives us the ability to stand! When we get to this powerful place, the throne of grace, we will also receive His mercy, forgiveness, and the desire and power to do His will!

So, why are YOU turning back? What is causing you to drift away? There's no need to drift away because Jesus is the better sacrifice! There is no greater love, than His love! Instead, we must take heed to the warnings of the danger of neglecting the gift of salvation, the danger of unbelief, the danger of not maturing, and the danger of falling away! The author is challenging us to draw near to God with a sincere heart in full assurance of faith, having our hearts sprinkled to cleanse us from a guilty conscience and having our bodies washed with pure water.

The Lord is calling us out of a place of complacency, to a place of consciousness! He is challenging our awareness of the spiritual things that are set before us. We cannot live in a sedated state, but in an active faith, that can successfully move mountains. Now is the time to overcome the fear of persecution, shame, and doubt. Our distractions come in all shapes and sizes and from every direction. Paul tells us that we can no longer allow ourselves to be tossed to and fro as children. We must mature in the things of God and not keep starting over! The threat of persecution, shame or doubt will not take us out! Remember, Jesus says, to touch not my anointed. Isaiah 54:17 says, "No weapon formed against you is going to prosper, and you will refute every tongue that accuses you. This is the heritage of the servants of the Lord, and this is their vindication from me!" The Hebrews author says; "we are not of those who draw back! Those that retreat are of destruction and will be destroyed! But those who believe will be saved" (Hebrews 10:39). We are covered by the Spirit of the Lord. He is our Protector! You can't give in, not NOW!

This transition is not just from a physical place. Although you may have the vision of something tangible, this is not the move that He is bringing you into right now. Before God can move you physically, He desires to move you spiritually into His house, His kingdom. He has to know that your faith is firmly planted, believing and trusting in Him as the crucified and risen Savior. He needs to know that your faith includes you being obedient to His Word, as a way of life, not a temporary moment! You must be set apart from your former life and committed to your life in Christ. "Choose you this day whom you will serve." (Joshua 24:15)

"Now faith (our firm belief and trust in Christ, the crucified and risen Savior)," is the substance of things hoped for! The Holy Spirit is moving you from a place of weakness to a place of spiritual maturity; from a place of neglect and falling away to a place of assurance, confidence and a place of righteousness! Your change is inevitable unless you are still dull of hearing, and your heart continues to be hardened. If that is the case,

I pray right now that you are freed from any rebellious spirits holding you and that your heart will be opened to allow the Holy Spirit to do work within you. Moreover, that you're released from any hurt, pain, strife, envy, resentment and bitterness to receive the grace that God has bestowed upon you. Satan, we come against your accusations and your attacks. We already know that you are the father of Lies, wicked and deceitful. We cast you out right now! At this specific moment, we come in agreement with this person who is walking by faith and not by sight! We are unlocking the hold that you've had and receiving them in the love of Jesus Christ and the sweet communion of the Holy Spirit. We command you, Satan, to cease. We come boldly to the throne of grace, and we receive His mercy to help us in our time of trouble. We thank you, God for answering our prayers, in Jesus name we prayer, Amen!

Hallelujah, thank you, Jesus, for your eternal power working in our lives! In my spirit, I'm singing the chorus of this hymn, "My Faith Looks Up to Thee," I believe it's a testimony:

"My faith looks up to Thee, Thou Lamb of Calvary. Savior divine! Now hear me while I pray. Take all my guilt away, Oh let me from this day be wholly Thine! May Thy rich grace imparts Strength to my fainting heart, my zeal inspire! As Thou has died for me, O may my love to Thee, pure, warm, and changeless be, a living fire!

I hear the cry of the psalmist petitioning God with his faith. Wanting God to hear his prayer; asking Him to take all of his guilt away, and let him be completely His. He acknowledges the grace that is coming from God that will strengthen his fainting heart and fuel his zeal of inspiration. Yes, Christ has died for him, and he now wants his love for God to be pure, warm, and changeless; a living fire!

Can you say, "My faith looks up to thee?" Or, "that your love for the one true God is pure, warm, and changeless, a living fire?" I need you to be honest with yourself. There's no one here to impress! It's just you and your inner man!

"Now unto to Him, who is able to keep you from stumbling; And to present you faultless before His presence of His glory, with exceeding joy. To God our Savior, who alone is wise, be glory and majesty, dominion and power, both NOW and forever, Amen." (Jude 24-25)

Go in peace, Believing Beyond

From this day, forward!

My Story...

My voice...

"I've come this far by faith!" From my child-hood to my adult life, I can recall singing this hymn in our church services. Every Sunday, the choirs would make a processional into the sanctuary, singing, "We've come this far by faith; leaning on the Lord. Trusting in His holy word; He never failed me yet!" Hearing these words now, bring more meaning than when I was growing up. Back then, I didn't re-late to it emotionally, mentally or spiritually. The essence of this hymn once eluded me, but now, it seems to be the glue to my spiritual ex-istence. I'm convinced that the Lord has never left me, and it is by His grace that He kept me. So, I'm singing louder than ever, "We've come this far by faith!

Today's faith is different from yester-day's faith because I believe that He does ex-ceeding and abundantly above anything that I can think or even ask (Ephesians 3:20). Yes-terday my faith was limited to the confines of what people said that I could do, and I limited myself to what I thought I had the ability to do, on my own. I also believed that I would not accomplish the spiritual things that God had ordained for me to do! I was not the person I saw in my spiritual vision.

Now, what I know for sure is that everything that I have been through has a divine blessing attached! When I felt alone, and it didn't look like I would ever make it, God still had a plan for me. He cared for me, and I belonged to Him. My dark days were the days that I needed more of His light to see my way through. The lonely days were the days that I needed His unconditional love surrounding me. The painful days were the days that I felt His presence healing me. There was nothing that I experienced that He could not and would not bring me through. The lesson learned is that He will never leave me nor forsake me. I had to grow in faith to trust Him with my whole heart and believe that He would deliver me out of all my afflictions. The more I believed that He would deliver me, the more He allowed me to see His awesomeness in my life!

Because I was willing to face my afflictions through my faith in Him, His power, presence and purpose dwelled richly in me. I was convinced by the work of the Holy Spirit, that I was being refined and reformed into a Woman of God. I was ready, willing and able to do the work of the ministry. In 1988, the Lord had given me a vision of the ministry I was to do! I spent so many years searching for the manifestation of the ministry. I searched outside of myself, only to learn that the purpose that He ordained for me lived inside of me! I doubted my place in the kingdom of God. I thought I needed to be "right," to do what He was calling me to do! "Being right," is still a work in progress, but being saved and believing that He can "really" do all things, makes the difference.

My faith caused me to come out from among them! It called me out of my hiding place. I could no longer hide behind people, places or things. I could not let those that I thought were better, smarter, more gifted or even more anointed intimidate the Spirit that was roaring on the inside. My trumpet was sounding! "The Spirit of the Lord is upon me." (Isaiah 61:1) He has clothed me with His garments of salvation and clothed me with His robe of righteousness.

I am free, praise the Lord, I'm free! No longer bound, no more chains holding me. My soul is resting; it's such a blessing! Praise the Lord, Hallelujah, I'm free. By faith, I have recognized my distractions were just distractions, and they no longer have authority over me! Therefore, I was released to move into the spiritual authority that the Lord has called forth.

He has called me to open the blinded eyes, to turn them from the darkness to the light. From the power of Satan to the power of God (Isaiah 61:2). It is His power that has prepared and sanctioned me to do the work. The presence of the Lord keeps me encouraged to keep doing the work He has assigned for me to do.

What God has done for me, is the same thing that He's willing to do for whoever is willing to let Him do what He does. The hymn says, "We've come this far by faith, leaning on the Lord!" Not only did I lean on Him, I totally relied on His promises. Often it has been His strength and not mine!

The gift we are all given is the gift of faith! Remember, "Faith is the substance of the things we are hoping for and the evidence of the things not seen." (Hebrews 11:1) With our faith, we now have the ability to overcome every obstacle and trap the enemy has set before us. We are no longer unequally yoked to anything that is unpleasing to the Lord. Miracles are being performed right now, on your behalf, by the power of His Holy Spirit. Your faith will cause you to produce the fruit of the Spirit, in your personal life. It is bringing forth God's love (that is unconditional), His joy (that is unbreakable), His peace (that surpasses all understanding), His longsuffering (that makes us tolerant), His kindness (a spirit of compassion), His faithfulness (shows dependability), His gentleness (the ability to love), and His self-control (the willpower)!

The willpower to overcome is promised to all who believe. Jesus says, "He that hath an ear, let him hear what the Spirit is saying to the church."(Revelation 2:7) Overcoming is essential to living in Christ. Satan wants to destroy you, but God has a plan to deliver you.

It's only by faith that we can stamp out the attack of the enemy. Choose you this day, whom you will serve. As for me and my house, we will serve the Lord." (Joshua 24:15)

JESUS IS THE BREAD OF LIFE! HE IS OUR SUSTAINER! HE IS THE GIVER OF LIFE, TO A MORE ABUNDANT LIFE!

Believing Beyond will bring you into your divine destiny! It will push you past the limitations of your imagination. Believing Beyond will release any strongholds that have been holding you back from moving forward. Believing Beyond is your opportunity to walk through the open door that God has set before you, that no man can shut (Revelaion 3:8)! It's not about a title or position; it's about your faith that He is the Messiah, the King of Kings, and the Lord of Lords.

The chorus says Oh, oh, oh, can't turn around; we've come this far by faith. As I look back, there is evidence that it's only by my faith in God that I am sharing my story and writing this book. So many times I wanted to turn around and give up, but my faith sustained me. No matter how difficult my life experiences were, the Holy Spirit was always present to give me a place of refuge and a place of peace. So now, I'm "Believing Beyond......" Will you join me?

Believing Beyond!

Made in the USA
Middletown, DE
21 March 2024

51359159R00066